What Happens After Life?

RON RHODES

HARVEST HOUSE PUBLISHERS
EUGENE, OREGON

Cover by Dugan Design Group, Bloomington, Minnesota

Cover photo © Anastasios Kandris / Shutterstock

WHAT HAPPENS AFTER LIFE?
Copyright © 2014 by Ron Rhodes
Published by Harvest House Publishers
Eugene, Oregon 97402
www.harvesthousepublishers.com

Library of Congress Cataloging-in-Publication Data
    Rhodes, Ron.
    What Happens After Life? / Ron Rhodes.
       pages cm
    ISBN 978-0-7369-5138-8 (pbk.)
    ISBN 978-0-7369-5139-5 (eBook)
    1. Future life—Christianity—Meditations. 2. Heaven—Christianity—Meditations. I. Title.
    BT903.R46 2014
    236'.2—dc23

                                                            2013013818

Printed in the United States of America

14 15 16 17 18 19 20 21 22 / BP-JH / 10 9 8 7 6 5 4 3 2

Acknowledgments

Thanks, Mom and Dad. I often found myself thinking of you and smiling as I wrote this book. I look forward to seeing you again in the heavenly country!

Thanks, Kerri. I cannot imagine a more perfect wife and life companion. You are an endless source of blessing to me. Our life together has been and continues to be a joy as we travel hand in hand to the heavenly country.

Thanks, David and Kylie. You are both such a joy to your mother and me. You are loved more than words can express.

Thanks, Harvest House Publishers. I'm so glad we are partnering together on yet another book. (How many has it been now?) I consider it a privilege to work with you.

Thanks, faithful readers. I so appreciate the blessing and honor of being able to share and explore the Scriptures with you for these many years.

Most important, thank You, Lord Jesus. Serving You is the single greatest privilege and joy I've ever known. You are awesome and are truly worthy to be praised. Thank You for preparing a place for me in heaven. I so look forward to the rapture!

Contents

Introduction: Timeless Truths About Heaven
and the Afterlife 7

1. An Appointed Time to Die 9
2. Death: A Transition into the Afterlife 15
3. The Intermediate State 23
4. The Rapture: A Rendezvous with the Lord in the Air 31
5. Resurrection Bodies with "Permaflesh" 39
6. Christians at the Judgment Seat of Christ 47
7. New Heavens and a New Earth 57
8. The New Jerusalem: The Eternal City 65
9. No More Sin, Mourning, Pain, Tears, or Death 75
10. Satan and Demons Eternally Quarantined 81
11. Earthly Realities Absent in Heaven 89
12. Face-to-Face Fellowship with God 97
13. A Reunion of Christian Loved Ones 103
14. Meaningful Activities in Heaven 109
15. No Need to Fear Death 115
16. Heaven for Infants and Young Children Who Die 121
17. Assessing Personal Visits to Heaven 129
18. Unbelievers at the Great White Throne Judgment 137
19. Unbelievers and Eternal Suffering 143
20. No Second Chance After Death 151
21. Hooking Our Hope in Heaven 157

Bibliography 165
Notes 167

Introduction:

Timeless Truths About Heaven and the Afterlife

Life on earth is short. Life in heaven is long. (It is eternal.) It therefore makes good sense for Christians to take a little time to ponder timeless truths about heaven and the afterlife. Put another way, we Christians are wise to live our short lives on earth in view of our imminent transition to our long lives in heaven.

You are not holding a dry and dusty book of theology in your hands. Rather, you are holding a book of devotional and inspirational truths you can apply to your life. This kind of theology is engineered to make a difference in the way you live your Christian life. These truths are not just for the head but also for the heart. Theology that does not touch the heart—that fails to resonate with your inner spirit so that it changes you—has failed at its task. That's one reason I'm excited about this book. My prayer is that it will cause a paradigm shift in the way you view this present world. The more your present life is informed by the glorious truths of heaven, the more you will gain an eternal perspective that will help you navigate the difficult circumstances you might face in life.

You will notice that this book has 21 chapters. Each chapter is short enough to read in a day. If you follow this route, you will join me for a three-week tour of the afterlife. However, feel free to take things slower if you wish. The timeless truths in most of these chapters are too important, too spiritually rich and uplifting, to rush through. I urge you to allow each truth to yield its full blessing as you relax and meditate on it. Don't let the tyranny of the urgent rob you of the blessing.

Even the chapters on unbelievers, their judgment, and their eternal destiny can yield some benefit to us. First, these chapters help us to clearly see what Jesus Christ has rescued us from in the salvation He has provided for us. Second, these chapters motivate us to share the good news of Jesus with unbelievers so that they too can go to heaven. Third, these chapters help us to understand why evildoers must be eternally quarantined from believers in the afterlife. Without such a quarantine, the spread of evil would continue endlessly.

So, my friend, let's dive into the Scriptures. And let's be open-minded about what God wants to teach us. Let's resolve to allow God to do His life-changing work in us as His Word saturates our hearts and minds.

> FATHER, *I pray that as my readers journey through this book,*
> *You will bring spiritual blessing and enrichment to them.*
> *By Your Spirit, open their eyes so they may behold wondrous*
> *things in Your Word. May Your Word bring revival to their souls.*
> *May the joy of the Lord be their strength. Please give them an*
> *eternal, top-down perspective that enables them to see all earthly*
> *realities and problems from the vantage point of heaven.*
> *I pray in Jesus's blessed name. Amen.*

1

An Appointed Time to Die

While I was writing this book, a 21-year-old boy who had been a longtime acquaintance of our family was in a fatal automobile accident. He attended the same Christian university my two children attended. After visiting some friends one evening, he was driving home but was going a bit too fast. He suddenly came upon some garbage cans in the road, which caused him to swerve, lose control, and then hit a tree. It all happened terribly fast. In the hours past midnight, after the police had sorted everything out, there was a knock at the door of his parents' house. The police on the doorstep informed them of the tragic accident.

We were all deeply saddened to hear about the accident. We took comfort, however, in the reality that this young man was a Christian and that he was now in the presence of his Savior, Jesus the Messiah. His funeral celebrated his life and truly honored the Lord Jesus.

From a human perspective, many would say that this young man died before his time or suffered a premature death. From a biblical perspective, however, God has appointed each one of us a certain amount of time to dwell on the earth. Even before we were born, God in His sovereignty and infinite wisdom determined the exact time allotment for each one of us. Some of us die very young. Others die at a ripe old age. But in every case, the time we have on earth is precisely what God long ago determined for each of us. There are thus no premature deaths in God's sovereign timetable.

All of Scripture points to God's sovereign oversight of the timing of life and death for every person. In Job 14:5, for example, we are told that a human being's "days are determined." The Hebrew word for "determined" in this verse carries the idea of something being engraved on stone. We might think of our time allotment on earth as being set in concrete by God. Our time allotment is a sure thing. We cannot die sooner than God's appointed time for us, nor can we live longer than God's appointed time for us.

This verse also affirms, "The number of his months is with you" (that is, with God). This is a simple way of saying that the number of our months is under God's sovereign control and oversight. Job continues, "You have appointed his limits that he cannot pass."

We also see this reality in Psalm 139:16, where the psalmist affirmed to God, "In your book were written, every one of them, the days that were formed for me, when as yet there was none of them." Some scholars suggest that the book (or more literally, the scroll) referenced here may be the "book of the living"—God's royal register mentioned in Psalm 69:28 (see also Exodus 32:32-33). Regardless, it seems clear from this verse that our allotment of time on earth—"every one of" our days—was sovereignly determined by God before we were even born.

Acts 17:26 likewise informs us that God "made from one man every nation of mankind to live on all the face of the earth, having determined allotted periods and the boundaries of their dwelling place." God thus not only sovereignly determines how long each individual will live but also how long each nation will survive (see Daniel 2:36-45; Luke 21:24). As Bible expositor Thomas Constable has put it, God "determines the times of nations—their seasons, when they rise and fall—and their boundaries."[1]

God Is Sovereign over All Things

The broader backdrop to God's sovereignty over the timing of human death is that God is sovereign over all things in the universe. God rules the universe, controls all things, and is Lord over all (Ephesians 1). Nothing can happen in this universe that is beyond the reach of His control. All forms of existence are within the scope of His absolute dominion.

Psalm 66:7 affirms that He "rules by his might forever." God asserts, "My counsel shall stand, and I will accomplish all my purpose" (Isaiah 46:10). God assures us, "As I have planned, so shall it be, and as I have purposed, so shall it stand" (Isaiah 14:24).

Proverbs 16:9 tells us, "The heart of man plans his way, but the LORD establishes his steps." Proverbs 19:21 says, "Many are the plans in the mind of a man, but it is the purpose of the LORD that will stand." As applied to the issue of death, it is clear that regardless of how long we may plan to live, how long we think we might live, or how long insurance companies expect us to live, God alone ultimately makes that determination. Theologian Paul Enns explains:

> God directs our lives, all the details, event after event, year after year, and then at precisely the right time, He takes us home. God determines the number of days we spend on earth. They are different for each of us. Some live longer lives, some shorter. Then, at the end of our days, He receives us home, into the brilliance of His heavenly home. [2]

Human Life Is Short

Whether God's sovereign allotment of time for us involves few years or many years—whether we die as children or in old age—human life often seems all too short, especially from the perspective of eternity. This reality is reflected throughout both the Old and New Testaments.

In Job 14:1 we read that "man who is born of a woman is few of days and full of trouble." Job therefore urged God, "Remember that my life is a breath" (Job 7:7). The psalmist likewise affirmed to God, "Behold, you have made my days a few handbreadths, and my lifetime is as nothing before you. Surely all mankind stands as a mere breath!" (Psalm 39:5). "Man is like a breath; his days are like a passing shadow" (Psalm 144:4). The psalmist laments, "My days pass away like smoke" (Psalm 102:3). Just as a puff of smoke quickly disperses in the air and disappears, so human life seems to vanish all too quickly.

In the New Testament, James, well aware of this Old Testament teaching, urges, "You do not know what tomorrow will bring. What is your life? For you are a mist that appears for a little time and then vanishes" (James 4:14). This verse presents three notable realities.

1. We appear (that is, we are born).
2. We live for a short time.
3. We then vanish (that is, we physically die).

Peter expresses the same truth with a metaphor of grass and flowers: "All flesh is like grass and all its glory like the flower of grass. The grass withers, and the flower falls" (1 Peter 1:24). This verse finds ample illustration in our own lives, does it not? All we need to do is pull out a few photo albums and see what we looked like five years ago, ten years ago, or twenty years ago. The "glory" does indeed fade fast.

Even if we do all we can to take care of ourselves, we'll still eventually die. No matter how healthy the foods we eat, no matter how vigorous our exercise program, no matter how many vitamins we take, and no matter how low our cholesterol may be, we will still die.

We Do Not Know the Day of Our Death

God sovereignly knows the exact year, month, day, minute, and second of our death, but you and I are unaware of God's chosen time. This, too, is often reflected in the pages of Scripture.

- When Isaac was a very old man, he mused: "Behold, I am old; I do not know the day of my death" (Genesis 27:2).
- The writer of Ecclesiastes laments, "Man does not know his time. Like fish that are taken in an evil net, and like birds that are caught in a snare, so the children of man are snared at an evil time, when it suddenly falls upon them" (9:12).

Death often comes suddenly and with little or no warning, as it did with our 21-year-old friend who died.

What Should Our Attitude Be?

What should be our attitude in view of the short time we have on earth? Scripture provides the answer.

1. Our days are limited, so we ought to live each day to the fullest and be mindful of living for the Lord 24/7. The psalmist prayed, "O LORD, make me know my end and what is the measure of my days; let me know how fleeting I am!" (Psalm 39:4). An awareness of mortality instills in us a desire to make every day count.

2. Though our mortal bodies age and become progressively weaker over time, our spiritual nature is renewed day by day as we walk with God. As 2 Corinthians 4:16 puts it, "We do not lose heart. Though our outer self is wasting away, our inner self is being renewed day by day." So regardless of your age, keep your focus on spending time in Scripture and walking with God. Keep the things of the Spirit at the top of your priorities.

3. We ought to never be presumptuous of a long life, for that is not a guarantee. Proverbs 27:1 tells us, "Do not boast about tomorrow, for you do not know what a day may bring." We have seen that James wrote a similar New Testament exhortation (James 4:14).

4. Scripture reveals that people who obey and honor the Lord live longer, while those who dishonor Him may find their lives being cut short. Proverbs 10:27 tells us that "the fear of the LORD prolongs life, but the years of the wicked will be short." Indeed, "the fear of the LORD is a fountain of life, that one may turn away from the snares of death" (Proverbs 14:27). Deuteronomy 4:40 instructs, "You shall keep his statutes and his commandments…that it may go well with you and with your children after you, and that you may prolong your days in the land that the LORD your God is giving you for all time." In the New Testament, Paul writes, "Honor your father and mother…that it may go well with you and that you may live long in the land" (Ephesians 6:2-3). Long life goes hand in hand with living one's life according to God's ways (see Proverbs 3:16; 4:10; 9:11).

Scripture includes at least one case of God extending a righteous man's life. I am speaking of Hezekiah. The prophet Isaiah had informed the gravely ill Hezekiah that he would soon die. But then Hezekiah prayed, "O LORD, please remember how I have walked before you in faithfulness and with a whole heart, and have done what is good in your sight." God subsequently added 15 years to Hezekiah's life (2 Kings 20:3-6). Living in righteousness definitely pays off!

Wisdom to Remember

- God has appointed each one of us a certain amount of time to dwell on this earth, after which time we will certainly die.

- God is sovereign over all things in the universe, so it makes good sense that He is also sovereign over the precise day of our death.

- Human life seems all too short. The days pass all too quickly.

- None of us are aware of the precise time we will die.

- We ought therefore to make every day count for the Lord, make our spiritual lives a high priority, avoid being presumptuous of a long life, and daily seek to honor the Lord in all things. Doing these things can lead to long life.

OUR FATHER, *You are truly wondrous before our eyes. In Your matchless wisdom, You have given each of us a different allotment of time on earth. For some of us, the years are few, and for others, many. But in each case, our time allotment is from You. Father, may our awareness of our mortality motivate us to live each precious remaining day with You, knowing that one day we will be face to face with You. Let us not fear death, but rather perpetually recognize that through Christ, the sting has been taken out of death. Let us be mindful that death for Christians involves an instant transition into Your presence in heaven. Thank You, Lord, for the gift of time. May we all use it wisely.*

2

Death: A Transition
into the Afterlife

I'm writing only a few months after Chuck Colson died. I remember when I first met Colson. I was a cohost of a local radio show in Houston, Texas, called *Carpool*. This show aired during the morning commute. We recorded the show in a studio, but we had street sounds playing in the background as if we were driving to work as we did the broadcast.

During the *Carpool* radio broadcast, we'd typically have someone "along for the ride." We'd talk as if we were picking someone up on the street corner. On this one particular day, we "picked up" Chuck Colson. We felt honored to interview him about his then-recent book, *Born Again*.

After Colson died, it struck me that it doesn't matter whether you're famous or completely unknown, rich or poor, male or female, tall or short, with light skin or dark skin. All people eventually die—with the sole exception of those Christians who will be alive on earth at the time of the rapture (1 Thessalonians 4:13-17). As Hebrews 9:27 tells us, "It is appointed for man to die once, and after that comes judgment."

On April 21, 2012, Colson's earthly sojourn ended. The good news, however, is that he instantly transitioned into heaven! His spirit left his body as easily as a hand slips out of a glove, and the angels escorted his spirit directly into Christ's presence in heavenly paradise (see Luke 16:22). The same will be true of you and me when we die.

2

Famous Last Words

I've always been fascinated by people's last words. The things people say right before they die reveal a great deal about how they view life, death, and their belief about life after death.[1]

General John Sedgwick, a Union Army general in the American Civil War, said this the instant before his death in 1864: "Don't worry boys…They couldn't hit an elephant at this dist—" An enemy bullet struck him at that fatal moment, and he immediately died in the presence of his men. If we learn one thing from Sedgwick, it's that death often comes unexpectedly.

A doctor attempted to comfort Ethan Allen, a Revolutionary War general, by saying, "General, I fear the angels are waiting for you." Allen replied, "Waiting are they? Waiting are they? Well, let 'em wait"— and then a moment later, he died. It seems obvious that Allen was not anticipating a glorious existence in heaven following the moment of death. He was doing all he could to hold on to the faint glimmer of life remaining in him.

Louis B. Mayer, the famous American film producer with Metro-Goldwyn-Mayer (MGM), said at the moment of his death in 1957, "Nothing matters…nothing matters." This seems to be a cry of despondency. His dying words illustrate the primary truth of the book of Ecclesiastes: Without God in one's life, all is futile; all is meaningless (Ecclesiastes 1:2). Death is the end.

Voltaire, a French Enlightenment writer, historian, and philosopher who died in 1778, said to his doctor in his last moments of life, "I wish I had never been born." He implored his doctor, "I will give you half of what I am worth if you will give me six more months of life." Here is a man who had no hope of an afterlife.

Several famous philosophers seemed rather uncertain about what lies beyond death's door. Philosopher Thomas Hobbes, who died in 1679, uttered right before he passed, "I am about to take my last voyage, a great leap in the dark." French philosopher François Rabelais, who died in 1553, was likewise heard to say right before the moment of death, "I am going to the great Perhaps." This same kind of uncertainty permeates much of our current world.

Other people who have died expressed an ignorance of their mortal danger following death. Charles Darwin, the founder of the evolutionary hypothesis who died in 1882, was heard to say right before death, "I am not the least afraid to die." He had no sense of accountability to a Creator following death.

Many people have false hopes about what lies beyond death's door. Saddam Hussein, who was executed by hanging in 2006, said right before his death, "There is no God but Allah, and Muhammad is God's messenger." Hussein had firm hopes of going to the Muslim paradise. In the Muslim view, paradise is a sensual place of pleasure, where faithful men can have 72 beautiful maidens at their disposal and eat and drink and enjoy full bodily satisfaction. Instead, Hussein entered into a Christless eternity with a destiny in the lake of fire.

I shudder to think of what it might be like for those (like Hussein) who reject Christ but nevertheless expect a wondrous afterlife. Suddenly, when the moment of death falls, they discover their true destiny. What a ruinous awakening it must be.

How different it is for those who truly love Jesus. John Wesley, the founder of Methodism who died in 1791, said right before he passed, "The best of all is: God is with us." He knew that the Christian does not go through death alone. As the psalmist said so long ago, "Even though I walk through the valley of the shadow of death, I will fear no evil, for you are with me" (Psalm 23:4). Bible expositor J. Vernon McGee reflects Wesley's sentiments:

> Our human family lives in the shadow of death. When a person is born, he starts down a great canyon, and that canyon is the valley of the shadow of death...But, all the while I walk through that valley, I will fear no evil...We can know that our Shepherd is with us at all times, and even at the time of death.[2]

John Wesley's mother, Susanna, said right before her passing in 1742, "Children, when I am gone, sing a song of praise to God." Why sing a song of praise? Simply because at the moment of death, the Christian's spirit departs the physical body and enters directly into heaven in the presence of Jesus (2 Corinthians 5:8; Philippians 1:21-23). Glorious!

This fact caused missionary David Brainerd, at the moment of his death in 1747, to say, "I am going into eternity, and it is sweet for me to think of eternity." He knew where he was going once his earthly life was over.

My friends, the issue of death is profoundly relevant for each one of us. As one of my colleagues said tongue-in-check, "The current death rate is one hundred percent." Currently, 3 people die every second. That's 180 people every minute, 10,800 people every hour, and 259,200 every day. A headline on an Internet site read, "Death: The Nation's #1 Killer."

You and I live in local cities. As we go about our daily business, we may hear news about the deaths of some famous people as well as people in our communities. But we are generally unaware of the staggering number of deaths worldwide. We live in small bubbles that insulate us from these gruesome statistics. The truth is, though, that souls are flying out of bodies day in and day out on planet earth. Death is pervasive, and none of us know when the actual moment of death will arrive. That is why we must all be ready before it does.

Biblical Attitudes About Death

In Scripture, death shapes people's view of life. In 1 Kings 2:1-2, for example, we read, "When David's time to die drew near, he commanded Solomon his son, saying, 'I am about to go the way of all the earth. Be strong, and show yourself a man.'" "The way of all the earth" is a way of describing the reality that all people die. No one is exempt.

Joshua, when he was old, used similar terminology when sharing some final words with his people: "Now I am about to go the way of all the earth, and you know in your hearts and souls, all of you, that not one word has failed of all the good things that the LORD your God promised concerning you. All have come to pass for you; not one of them has failed" (Joshua 23:14). Again, "the way of all the earth" points to the reality that all people die. But Joshua also mentions that God fulfills His promises. As we'll see throughout the rest of this book, God will certainly fulfill all His promises to Christians regarding what lies in store for us in the afterlife.

Sometimes in the Old Testament, the reality of death is described in terms of absolute finality. Job, for example, lamented, "As the cloud fades and vanishes, so he who goes down to Sheol does not come up" (Job 7:9). (Sheol was considered the habitat of the dead in Old Testament times.) Job also said, "For when a few years have come I shall go the way from which I shall not return" (Job 16:22). Death is final!

Yet the Old Testament also recognized that at death, a believer is reunited with other believers who have already passed on from earth. For example, when Ishmael was 137 years old, "he breathed his last and died, and was gathered to his people" (Genesis 25:17).

Similarly, Genesis 49:33 tells us, "When Jacob finished commanding his sons, he drew up his feet into the bed and breathed his last and was gathered to his people."

When we get to the New Testament, we find increased clarity on issues related to death and the afterlife. In fact, the apostle Paul reveals that death is a mere transition into the afterlife. Paul could hardly wait to get to heaven.

> For to me to live is Christ, and to die is gain. If I am to live in the flesh, that means fruitful labor for me. Yet which I shall choose I cannot tell. I am hard pressed between the two. My desire is to depart and be with Christ, for that is far better. But to remain in the flesh is more necessary on your account (Philippians 1:21-24).

Paul's desire was to die so that his spirit could depart from his earthly body and go to be with Jesus in heaven. As Bible expositor Warren Wiersbe put it, "When Christ is your life, death is not your enemy; and you have the assurance of being with Christ when life ends." [3]

Paul was apparently speaking from experience, for earlier in his ministry he had actually been caught up to heaven, and he witnessed it firsthand (see 2 Corinthians 12:2-4). He liked what he saw there and wanted to go back. That's why he stated, "We are of good courage, and we would rather be away from the body and at home with

the Lord" (2 Corinthians 5:8). Eighteenth-century Bible commenta-
tor John Gill urged, "It is this which supports and comforts the saints
under all their sorrows here, and which makes them meet death with
pleasure." [4] Death is not the end. It is a mere transition into the afterlife, into the very presence of Jesus!

Of course, the apostle Paul's death came soon enough. As his earthly
life was drawing to a close, Paul informed his young apprentice Timothy, "I am already being poured out as a drink offering, and the time of
my departure has come" (2 Timothy 4:6). That is, the time had come
for his spirit to depart from his physical body and go to heaven. Paul
was prepared for the moment. Theologian Paul Enns makes this note:

> When the apostle Paul wrote Second Timothy, he was only
> a month or two away from being executed by beheading—
> and he knew it. It was in that circumstance and mental
> framework that Paul wrote the confident, upbeat words,
> "The Lord will rescue me from every evil deed, and will
> bring me safely to His heavenly kingdom; to Him be the
> glory forever and ever. Amen" (2 Tim. 4:18). [5]

Paul had no doubt that the Lord would bring him into heaven at
the moment of his death. You and I can have that same assurance.

Are You Ready?

I was with both my father and my mother when they died. My
father was the first to die, and it was due to multiple organ failure. Years
later, my mother died from a MRSA infection in her lungs. My father
and mother died in the same bedroom in the same house.

How precious it was to be with both of them as their spirits departed
their earthly bodies and entered into heaven. As I beheld their still
physical bodies, it was more than apparent that they were no longer
there. They were now in heaven. Ever since, I have counted on the reality that one day we will be reunited (see 1 Thessalonians 4:13-17).

My mom and dad were ready for the moment. Are you and I?

One of the purposes of this book is to help you fully understand
everything you need to know about what happens after life. I pray that

you will gain a sense of readiness so that when the moment arrives, you'll truly be ready.

> OUR LOVING FATHER, *we live in a society that seems to deny death. Many people are utterly unprepared when the moment of death suddenly arrives. I ask that You give us great wisdom about the transitory nature of life. The days pass so quickly. Enable us, Father, to see our lives as gifts of time from You. Enable us to use that time responsibly. And most important, Lord, enable us all to see the utter importance of salvation in Jesus Christ. For without Christ, none of us could look forward to heaven. We praise You, Father, for the salvation You have provided for us.*

3

The Intermediate State

When I'm at a funeral, I hear family members deliver very touching eulogies, often through tears. In these eulogies, the departed loved one's strong faith in Christ is often addressed. Sometimes I hear a family member affirm that even though their loved one's body is being lowered into the grave, he or she now has a wonderful resurrection body in heaven.

Of course, I would never seek to correct a point of theology among the grieving at a funeral. The truth is, however, that we do not receive our resurrection bodies immediately upon death. In fact, Scripture is clear that Christians who have passed on await the future day of resurrection, which will be on the day of the rapture.

The rapture is that glorious event in which the dead in Christ will be resurrected and living Christians will be instantly translated into their resurrection bodies. Both groups will be caught up to meet Christ in the air and taken back to heaven (John 14:1-3; 1 Corinthians 15:51-54; 1 Thessalonians 4:13-17). It will be an awesome event.

Until the time of the rapture, however, believers who have died exist in what theologians call the *intermediate state*. The intermediate state is an in-between state—our existence in between the time our mortal bodies die on earth and the time we receive our permanent resurrection bodies at the rapture (see Revelation 6:9-11).

It is precisely here that we must think carefully, for a debate has arisen among many over whether Christians who die exist in a disembodied state (as spirits) in heaven, or whether they might be given temporary bodies that will be replaced with permanent resurrection bodies at the rapture. Devout Christians are on both sides of the debate.

Of course, it's a friendly debate—what you might call an in-house debate. But it's important for each of us to understand why people on each side believe the way they do. In the process of addressing both views, I'll also give you my humble verdict on the issue.

The Temporary Body View

Some Christians think that even though we do not receive our permanent resurrection bodies until the day of the rapture, we nevertheless receive temporary bodies at the moment of death. They are convinced that Scripture supports this viewpoint.

A popular passage among those who hold to this view is 2 Corinthians 5:1-4. This passage seems to indicate that once the earthly body (metaphorically referred to as a tent) dies, Christians will receive a resurrection body (metaphorically referred to as a building) in heaven. Some suggest that these temporary resurrection bodies might be similar to the humanlike bodies angels sometimes appear in when they visit earth (see Hebrews 13:2).

Another scriptural evidence sometimes cited in favor of this viewpoint is that some descriptions of believers in heaven seem to indicate they have bodies. For example, we read about some Christian martyrs who, after being killed on earth, are pictured in heaven conversing with God (Revelation 6:9-11). Some reason that since these martyrs are portrayed as wearing white robes, they must have bodies of some sort. How else could they wear these robes? And if they converse, don't they need physical vocal chords?

Likewise, in Luke 16:19-31, we read about a believer (Lazarus) and a nonbeliever (the rich man) who died and entered into the afterlife. This passage tells us that the rich man desired for his tongue to be cooled by Lazarus's finger dipped in water. Some Christians reason that it would be impossible for a tongue to be cooled by a finger dipped in water unless those in the afterlife have some kind of temporary bodies.

The Disembodied Spirit View

It is certainly possible that we will have temporary bodies once we die and go to heaven—bodies that precede our permanent resurrection bodies. Luke 16:19-31 is probably the best supportive evidence for this idea.

Based on the broader context of the whole of Scripture, however, I remain convinced that each of us will be a disembodied spirit once we pass through death's door. Let me summarize why I believe this.

First, I agree that 2 Corinthians 5:1-4 definitely teaches that after our earthly bodies ("tents") die, we'll be given resurrection bodies ("buildings"). But the text does not tell us when we'll receive those resurrection bodies. Warren Wiersbe explains it this way:

> When a believer dies, the body goes to the grave, but the spirit goes to be with Christ (Phil. 1:20–25). When Jesus Christ returns for His own, He will raise the dead bodies in glory, and body and spirit shall be joined together for a glorious eternity in heaven (1 Cor. 15:35–58; 1 Thess. 4:13–18).[1]

Moreover, we are explicitly told in 2 Corinthians 5:1 that our resurrection bodies (or "buildings") will be "eternal in the heavens." It is therefore impossible to view these "buildings" as temporary resurrection bodies. (How can a temporary body be eternal?) It seems clear that our permanent resurrection bodies are in view in the passage—bodies that we'll receive on the day of the rapture.

As well, 2 Corinthians 5:1-4 indicates that once we die and our spirits depart from the body, we will experience a sense of being "naked" (verse 3). The term "naked" is a metaphorical reference to being bodiless. Just as a body can be without clothes, so our spirits can be without bodies. We will be "unclothed" in the sense of not yet having a resurrection body (see verse 4). Our nakedness—our sense of being "unclothed"—will not be remedied until the day of the rapture, when we'll all receive our permanent resurrection bodies (1 Thessalonians 4:13-17). Then we'll never be "unclothed" again.

As for the martyrs of Revelation 6, note that the apostle John refers to "the souls of those who had been slain" (verse 9). Their bodies were still on earth (dead) while their souls were in heaven. Then, in verse 11, we are told that "they were each given a white robe." The text does not stipulate that they wore these robes, only that robes were given to them. Perhaps the robes were given to them in anticipation of their eventual resurrections.

It is also possible that the white robes are intended to be taken as symbolic. Keep in mind that the book of Revelation often uses symbols to communicate literal truth. John said the seven stars in Christ's right hand were the angels (or messengers) of the seven churches, and the seven lampstands were the seven churches (Revelation 1:20). The bowls full of incense were the prayers of the saints (5:8), and the waters were peoples and multitudes and nations and languages (17:15). In view of the preponderance of symbols in the book of Revelation, it may well be that the white robes of the martyrs symbolize that they are in heaven because they have been made holy (white, or purified) by the death of Christ on their behalf. Consequently, this passage cannot be taken as a definitive proof that people have temporary bodies following the moment of death. Nor does the fact that they converse prove they have temporary bodies, for angels (as invisible spirit beings) can certainly speak and be heard (see, for example, Revelation 21:9).

Death as a Departure

The Bible reveals that you and I have both a material and an immaterial nature or aspect. The material part of a human being is the body (see Genesis 2:7; 3:19). The immaterial part is the soul or spirit. "Soul" and "spirit" are often used interchangeably in Scripture. Man's entire immaterial part is called "soul" in 1 Peter 2:11 and "spirit" in James 2:26. They must therefore be identical.

This helps us to better understand what happens at the moment of death. At death, the spirit, or soul, slips out of the physical body (see Genesis 35:18; 2 Corinthians 5:8; Philippians 1:21-23). When this happens, the "clothing" of the body is no longer on the spirit, so we experience that sense of being naked that the apostle Paul talks about in 2 Corinthians 5.

Quite a number of verses in the Bible address the spirit departing from the body at death. Here is a sampling.

Ecclesiastes 12:7 tells us that at the moment of death, "the spirit returns to God who gave it." This obviously requires a departure of the spirit from the physical body.

When Jesus died on the cross, He said to the heavenly Father, "Into your hands I commit my spirit" (Luke 23:46). Jesus knew that His physical body was about to die. He knew that once He died, His spirit would depart the body. It is this spirit that He entrusted to the Father's safekeeping. In His case, three days passed before He was resurrected from the dead. This means that Jesus existed in a bodiless state for those three days, apparently in the direct presence of the Father in heaven.

Stephen was a firm believer in Jesus Christ. Even in the face of death, he would not deny his Lord. Some antagonists threw stones at him to kill him. Right before he died, he prayed, "Lord Jesus, receive my spirit" (Acts 7:59). Stephen knew his physical body was about to die. But he also knew that his spirit would survive death, departing from the body at that very moment. This is why he committed his spirit into the safekeeping of Jesus.

The apostle Paul was concise about what happens at the moment of death. In 2 Corinthians 5:8 he affirms, "We are of good courage, and we would rather be away from the body and at home with the Lord." A plain reading of this verse supports the idea that during the intermediate state, we will be bodiless—that is, we will exist as spirits in heaven. Later in life, right before he was put to death, Paul affirmed to his young apprentice Timothy, "The time of my departure has come" (2 Timothy 4:6).

The Intermediate State for Christians

The prospect of being "naked" (or without a resurrection body) for a while might be interpreted by some as undesirable. But Paul says that even without a resurrection body, being with Christ in heaven is better by far than life on earth. "We would rather be away from the body and at home with the Lord" (2 Corinthians 5:8). The Greek word for "with" in the phrase "at home with the Lord" suggests close (face-to-face) fellowship. It is a word used of intimate relationships.

Paul also claimed, "My desire is to depart and be with Christ, for that is far better" (Philippians 1:23). The Greek word for "depart" was used in New Testament times of being freed from chains. Here on earth, you and I are anchored to the hardships and heartaches of this life. In death, however, these chains are broken. We are set free for entry into heaven. At the moment of death, the spirit departs the physical body and goes directly into the presence of the Lord.

At the very moment of death, Christians will be in paradise. Recall that during his ministry, the apostle Paul was "caught up to the third heaven," or paradise (2 Corinthians 12:2-3). Jesus told the repentant thief on the cross right before he died, "Truly, I say to you, today you will be with me in Paradise" (Luke 23:43).

The word "paradise" literally means "garden of pleasure" or "garden of delight." While Paul was there, "he heard things that cannot be told, which man may not utter." Apparently this paradise of God is so resplendently glorious, so ineffable, so wondrous, that Paul was forbidden to say anything about it to those still in the earthly realm. Maybe this explains why Paul was so anxious to get back there (Philippians 1:21-23). And maybe this is why Paul affirmed that "no eye has seen, nor ear heard, nor the heart of man imagined, what God has prepared for those who love him" (1 Corinthians 2:9). Paradise will be awesome!

The Intermediate State for Nonbelievers

The intermediate state of believers is one of bliss and joy, but the intermediate state of nonbelievers is horrific to ponder. At the moment of death, nonbelievers go as disembodied spirits to a temporary place of suffering (Luke 16:19-31). There they await their future resurrection and judgment, with an eventual destiny in the lake of fire (Revelation 20:11-15).

The intermediate state of the ungodly dead is described in 2 Peter 2:9: "The Lord knows how to...keep the unrighteous under punishment until the day of judgment." The word "keep" in this verse is in the present tense, indicating that the wicked (nonbelievers) are held captive and punished continuously. Peter is portraying them as condemned prisoners being closely guarded in a spiritual jail while awaiting future sentencing and final judgment.

In Jesus's story of the rich man and Lazarus in the afterlife, we discern a number of sobering facts about nonbelievers in the afterlife:

- The wicked dead suffer in agony.
- No one can comfort the wicked dead in the afterlife.
- There is no possibility of the wicked dead leaving the place of torment.
- The wicked dead are entirely responsible for not having listened to the warnings of Scripture in time (while on earth).

Probably the worst torment the nonbeliever will experience will be the perpetual knowledge that he or she could have trusted in Christ and escaped punishment. Throughout the endless aeons and aeons of eternity, the nonbeliever will always know that he or she could have enjoyed a heavenly destiny by trusting in Christ on earth.

Punishment in the intermediate state, however, is only temporary. The wicked dead will eventually be resurrected (Acts 24:15) and then judged at the great white throne judgment, and then their eternal punishment will begin in the lake of fire (Revelation 20:11-15).

It is sobering to realize that Scripture represents the state of nonbelievers after death as a fixed state, and there is no second chance (Luke 16:19-31; John 8:21,24; 2 Peter 2:4,9; Jude 6-7,13). Once one has passed through the doorway of death, there are no further opportunities to repent and turn to Christ for salvation (Matthew 7:22-23; 10:32-33; 25:41-46). Woe to those who reject Christ in this life.

> OUR FATHER, *we are so grateful that the very moment we die,*
> *our spirits will be issued into Your presence in heaven. We are*
> *overjoyed that beginning at that moment, we will never again*

have to face sin, Satan, sorrow, or death. How wondrous it will be! We are especially thankful that the sacrifice of Jesus on Calvary's cross made all this possible for us. Thank You, Jesus! You have taken what is ours (our sin) so that You might give us what is Yours (eternal life). Truly You are worthy.

4

The Rapture: A Rendezvous with the Lord in the Air

The rapture is that glorious and imminent event in which two groups of Christians will instantly be caught up to meet Christ in the air. I am referring to dead and living Christians. The dead in Christ will be resurrected, and then living Christians will be instantly translated into their resurrection bodies. After both groups are caught up to meet Christ in the air, they will be taken back to heaven, never again to be separated from Christ (John 14:1-3; 1 Corinthians 15:51-54; 1 Thessalonians 4:13-17).

This means that one generation of Christians will never pass through death's door. They will be alive on earth one moment, and the next moment they will be instantly translated into their resurrection bodies and caught up to meet Christ in the air. What an awesome moment that will be! If you are a Christian, it is possible that you and I will be among the living who will be caught up together to meet the Lord above the earth. It could happen in our generation.

Let's explore what Scripture teaches about this wondrous event.

A Mystery

A mystery, in the biblical sense, is a truth that cannot be discerned simply by human investigation, but requires special revelation from God. Generally, this word refers to a truth that was unknown to people living in Old Testament times but is now revealed to humankind by

God (Matthew 13:17; Colossians 1:26). This is illustrated in a key verse about the rapture of the church.

> Behold! I tell you a mystery. We shall not all sleep, but we shall all be changed, in a moment, in the twinkling of an eye, at the last trumpet. For the trumpet will sound, and the dead will be raised imperishable, and we shall be changed. For this perishable body must put on the imperishable, and this mortal body must put on immortality. When the perishable puts on the imperishable, and the mortal puts on immortality, then shall come to pass the saying that is written: "Death is swallowed up in victory." "O death, where is your victory? O death, where is your sting?" (1 Corinthians 15:51-55).

Resurrection was certainly taught in Old Testament times (for example, Daniel 12:2). But the rapture of the church—in which both dead and living Christians put on that which is imperishable and immortal, instantly being caught up to meet the Lord in the air—is a mystery because it had never been revealed in Old Testament times. It was revealed for the first time in the New Testament. This new teaching is no doubt one of the reasons New Testament believers became so excited about Bible prophecy.

When Will the Rapture Occur?

Some Christians believe the rapture will take place in the middle of the tribulation period. Others place it toward the end or at the end of the tribulation period. I believe a literal interpretation of prophetic Scripture supports the idea that it occurs prior to any part of the tribulation period.

The theological backdrop hinges on the nature of the tribulation as a time of God's wrath and on the nature of the universal church. We know from Scripture that the tribulation will be a seven-year period during which God's wrath will be poured out on the world prior to the second coming of Jesus Christ (Revelation 6:17; 14:10,19; 15:1,7; 16:1). We also know from Scripture that the universal church is the

ever-enlarging body of born-again believers who comprise the body
of Christ. It came into being on the day of Pentecost and continues
growing today (see Acts 2; compare with 1:5; 11:15; 1 Corinthians 12:13).
Scripture reveals that at the rapture, prior to the beginning of this
period of wrath, both the dead members of this universal church and
those who are still alive will be caught up to meet the Lord in the air.
Here are the scriptural evidences for this view:

- No Old Testament passage on the tribulation mentions the
  church (Deuteronomy 4:29-30; Jeremiah 30:4-11; Daniel
  8:24-27; 12:1-2).

- No New Testament passage on the tribulation mentions the church (Matthew 13:30,39-42,48-50; 24:15-31;
  2 Thessalonians 2:1-11; Revelation 4–18).

- Scripture does say that some believers will live during
  the tribulation period (for example, Revelation 6:9-11).
  But these people apparently become believers sometime after the rapture, perhaps as a result of the ministry
  of God's two prophetic witnesses (Revelation 11) or the
  144,000 Jewish evangelists (Revelation 7; 14).

- Scripture promises that the church is not appointed to
  wrath (Romans 5:9; 1 Thessalonians 1:9-10; 5:9). This
  means the church cannot go through the great day of
  wrath in the tribulation (Revelation 6:17).

- All throughout Scripture God is seen protecting His
  people before His judgment falls (see 2 Peter 2:5-9).
  Enoch was transferred to heaven before the judgment of
  the flood. Noah and his family were in the ark before the
  judgment of the flood. Lot was taken out of Sodom before
  judgment was poured out on Sodom and Gomorrah. The
  firstborn among the Hebrews in Egypt were sheltered by
  the blood of the Paschal Lamb before judgment fell. The
  spies were safely out of Jericho and Rahab was secured
  before judgment fell on Jericho. So, too, will the church be

secured safely (by means of the rapture) before judgment falls in the tribulation.

- The church is promised to be kept from the "hour of trial that is coming on the whole world, to try those who dwell on the earth" (Revelation 3:10). This verse indicates that believers will be saved "out of" or "from" (Greek: *ek*) the actual time ("hour") of the tribulation. This is consistent with God's promise to deliver the church from the "wrath to come" (1 Thessalonians 1:10; 5:9).

In the Twinkling of an Eye

The apostle Paul describes the rapture as occurring "in a moment, in the twinkling of an eye" (1 Corinthians 15:52). This is Paul's way of demonstrating how brief the moment of the rapture will be. Bible expositor Thomas Constable notes that "the Greek word translated 'moment' or 'flash' (*atomos*) refers to an indivisible fragment of time. The blinking of an eye takes only a fraction of a second." [1]

Think about it. The bodily transformation that living believers will experience at the rapture will be nearly instantaneous. One moment they will be on earth in mortal bodies, probably engaged in some routine activity. The next moment they will meet Christ in the clouds, instantly transformed into their glorified resurrection bodies.

The Bride and the Bridegroom

Christ is often portrayed in Scripture as the bridegroom (John 3:29), and the church is portrayed as the bride of Christ (Revelation 19:7). The imagery of Hebrew weddings teaches us something important about the rapture. Hebrew weddings included three phases:

1. The bride was betrothed to the groom through a legal agreement between their parents.

2. The bridegroom later came to claim his bride after preparing a place for them to live.

3. Family and friends celebrated at a marriage feast lasting several days.

All three of these phases are seen in Christ's relationship to the church, or bride of Christ.

1. As individuals living during the church age come to salvation, under the Father's loving and sovereign hand, they become a part of the bride of Christ (the church).

2. The Bridegroom (Jesus Christ) comes to claim His bride at the rapture and takes His bride to heaven, where He has prepared a place in the Father's house (John 14:1-3). The actual marriage takes place in heaven prior to the second coming (Revelation 19:6-9).

3. The marriage supper of the Lamb follows the second coming, apparently taking place on earth at the beginning of the millennial kingdom, Christ's 1000-year kingdom on earth (compare with Matthew 22:1-14; 25:1-13).

Just as an engaged couple counts the days until their wedding, so each of us Christians ought to look forward with great anticipation to the day of the rapture. It is a sad commentary on the state of the church that so many Christians today seem to be lethargic when it comes to issues related to Bible prophecy!

The Blessed Hope

Scripture writers sometimes refer to the rapture of the church as the "blessed hope." This event is blessed in the sense that it fosters a sense of blessedness in the believer's heart. The term carries the idea of joyous anticipation. Believers can hardly wait for it to happen!

Titus 2:13 urges Christians to look for the "blessed hope, the appearing of the glory of our great God and Savior Jesus Christ." As one Bible expositor put it, "We are looking for Jesus Christ to return; this is our only hope and glory...Believers should always be expecting His return and live like those who will see Him face-to-face." [2]

At this momentous event the dead in Christ will be resurrected, and believers still alive on earth will be instantly translated into their resurrection bodies (see Romans 8:22-23; 1 Corinthians 15:51-58; Philippians 3:20-21; 1 Thessalonians 4:13-18; 1 John 3:2-3). These bodies will never again be subject to sickness, sorrow, pain, and death. While we live in this fallen world as pilgrims who are just passing through, we are empowered by this magnificent blessed hope.

Distinct from the Second Coming

There is a big difference between the rapture and the second coming of Christ. The rapture involves Christ coming *for* His saints in the air prior to the tribulation, whereas at the second coming, He will come *with* His saints to the earth to reign for a thousand years (Revelation 19:1–20:6). The fact that Christ comes with His holy ones (redeemed believers) at the second coming presumes they have been previously raptured. (He cannot come *with* them until He has first come *for* them.)

Moreover, every eye will see Jesus at the second coming (Revelation 1:7), but the rapture is never described as being visible to the whole world. Rather, both dead and living believers are instantly caught up to meet the Lord in the air, after which they are escorted back to heaven.

Christians meet Jesus in the air at the rapture (1 Thessalonians 4:13-17), but at the second coming, Jesus's feet touch the Mount of Olives (Zechariah 14:4). At the rapture, Christians are taken and unbelievers are left behind (1 Thessalonians 4:13-17), whereas at the second coming, unbelievers are taken away in judgment (Luke 17:34-36) and mortal believers remain to enter into Christ's millennial kingdom (Matthew 25:31-46).

At the rapture, Jesus will receive His bride, whereas at the second coming He will execute judgment (Matthew 25:31-46). The rapture will take place in the blink of an eye (1 Corinthians 15:52), whereas the second coming will be more drawn out, and every eye will see Him (Matthew 24:30; Revelation 1:7).

You can build up your faith by meditating on Scriptures dealing with both of these prophetic events.

Key Verses on the Rapture	Key Verses on the Second Coming
John 14:1-3	Daniel 2:44-45; 7:9-14; 12:1-3
Romans 8:19	Zechariah 12:10; 14:1-15
1 Corinthians 1:7-8; 15:51-53; 16:22	Matthew 13:41; 24:15-31; 26:64
Philippians 3:20-21; 4:5	Mark 13:14-27; 14:62
Colossians 3:4	Luke 21:25-28
1 Thessalonians 1:10; 2:19; 4:13-18; 5:9,23	Acts 1:9-11; 3:19-21
2 Thessalonians 2:1	1 Thessalonians 3:13
1 Timothy 6:14	2 Thessalonians 1:6-10; 2:3,8
2 Timothy 4:1,8	1 Peter 4:12-13
Titus 2:13	2 Peter 3:1-14
Hebrews 9:28	Jude 14-15
James 5:7-9	Revelation 1:7; 19:11–20:6; 22:7,12,20
1 Peter 1:7,13; 5:4	
1 John 2:28–3:2	
Jude 21	
Revelation 2:25; 3:10	

An Imminent Event

The term "imminent" literally means "ready to take place" or "impending." The New Testament teaches that the rapture is imminent—that is, there is nothing that must be prophetically fulfilled before the rapture occurs (see "Key Verses on the Rapture" in the chart above). The rapture is a "signless" event that can occur at any moment. This is in contrast to the second coming of Christ, which is preceded by many events in the seven-year tribulation (see Revelation 4–18).

Imminence is implied in the apostle Paul's words in Romans 13:11-12: "You know the time, that the hour has come for you to wake from sleep. For salvation is nearer to us now than when we first believed. The night is far gone; the day is at hand. So then let us cast off the works of darkness and put on the armor of light." The word "salvation" in this context must point to the rapture, for Paul refers to it as a specific future event. At the end of each day, the Christian is that much closer to the time when the rapture may occur.

Imminence is also implied in James 5:7-9:

> Be patient, therefore, brothers, until the coming of the Lord. See how the farmer waits for the precious fruit of the earth, being patient about it, until it receives the early and the late rains. You also, be patient. Establish your hearts, for the coming of the Lord is at hand. Do not grumble against one another, brothers, so that you may not be judged; behold, the Judge is standing at the door.

Living Expectantly

We have looked at a New Testament analogy that relates the rapture to ancient Jewish marriages. In biblical times, a betrothed woman would eagerly await the coming of her groom to take her away to his father's house in marriage celebration. During this time of anticipation, the bride's loyalty and fidelity to her groom were tested. She sought to live in purity, remaining faithful to her beloved one.

Likewise, as the bride of Christ (the church) awaits the coming of the messianic Groom, the church is motivated to live in purity and godliness until He arrives at the rapture. Just as a wife seeks to be loyal to her husband, so the church ought to seek purity in awaiting the coming of the divine Groom (see Romans 13:11-14; 2 Peter 3:10-14; and 1 John 3:2-3).

> Our Father, *we so look forward to the coming of Jesus at the rapture. We are thankful that at the moment of the rapture, we will all receive resurrection bodies that will never again grow old, get sick, or die. We are also thankful that when Jesus comes for us, He will take us to the place He has prepared in Your house. We will have perfect bodies in a perfect environment—in perfect fellowship with You.*

5

Resurrection Bodies
with "Permaflesh"

We've all seen the Energizer Bunny on TV. It keeps on going and going and going. But of course, batteries don't last forever. The energy begins to deplete, and the bunny will get slower and slower until it stops altogether.

We find a metaphor here for the human body. When we're young, we feel as if we can keep going and going and going. As we age, however, things begin to slow down. And eventually, we stop altogether—that is, we die.

If you're in your fifties, as I am, you might think back to things you used to be able to do easily when you were a teenager…hop a fence, jump down the stairs, or run uphill without getting too winded. Those were the days! If I tried to jump down the stairs today, someone would have to call 911—and pronto. Even if we eat well and take care of our bodies, they become progressively weaker. It happens to all of us.

The likelihood of developing illnesses also increases as we age—heart disease, high blood pressure, kidney problems, diabetes, and much more. I remember when my dad's kidneys failed and he had to have regular dialysis. I remember when my brother-in-law had a heart attack. We all longingly reflect on our childhood years, when we never had to worry about such matters. (The worst thing we had to worry about was occasionally going to the dentist.)

The good news that puts all this into perspective is that you and I as Christians will one day receive body upgrades that include what I call *permaflesh*. In other words, one day you and I will receive resurrection bodies that will never grow old, never deteriorate, never get sick, and never lack strength. Energy will never wane. Health will never be absent. Our perfect resurrection bodies will know no limitations. There will only be eternal vitality. Doctors and dentists will be out of a job in heaven!

This wondrous body upgrade is what I want to briefly address in this chapter. We begin with the recognition that Jesus is the One who has made it all possible for us.

It's All Because of Jesus

When it comes to our future resurrection from the dead, Jesus is on center stage. He is the reason you and I will one day receive body upgrades with permaflesh.

Recall that following the death of Lazarus, Jesus told Lazarus's sister, "I am the resurrection and the life. Whoever believes in me, though he die, yet shall he live" (John 11:25). To prove He had the authority to make such promises, Jesus promptly raised Lazarus from the dead! I can almost picture Jesus then asking the crowd, "Any questions about My claim to be the resurrection and the life? Is My meaning clear?"

On another occasion, Jesus affirmed, "This is the will of him who sent me, that I should lose nothing of all that he has given me, but raise it up on the last day. For this is the will of my Father, that everyone who looks on the Son and believes in him should have eternal life, and I will raise him up on the last day" (John 6:39-40).

Because of what Jesus accomplished on our behalf, we will be resurrected from the dead—just as He was. We can rest in the quiet assurance that even though our mortal bodies may pass away in death, turning to dust in the grave, they will be gloriously raised, never again to grow old and die. The weakness and frailty we presently sense in our mortal earthly bodies are only temporary conditions. With our future body upgrades with permaflesh, such frailty will forever be a thing of the past.

Raised Imperishable in Glory and Power

I love the way the apostle Paul describes our resurrection bodies, especially regarding how much better they will be than our present mortal bodies. "What is sown is perishable; what is raised is imperishable. It is sown in dishonor; it is raised in glory. It is sown in weakness; it is raised in power" (1 Corinthians 15:42-43).

Paul graphically contrasts our present earthly bodies and our future resurrection bodies. "What is sown is perishable" is a metaphorical reference to the burial of a dead body. Just as one sows a seed in the ground, so the mortal body is sown in the sense that it is buried in the ground. When our bodies are placed in the grave, they decompose and return to dust.

The exciting thing relates to what is raised out of the ground—the resurrection body, or our body upgrade. Paul notes that our present bodies will perish. They succumb to disease and death. As we live year to year, we constantly struggle to fight off dangerous infections. We do everything we can to stay healthy, but we nevertheless get sick. Worse yet, we all eventually die. It is just a matter of time.

Our body upgrades, however, will be imperishable. This means that all liability to disease and death will be forever gone. Never again will we have to worry about infections or passing away.

Paul then affirms that our present mortal body is "sown in dishonor; it is raised in glory." Of course, we rightfully try to honor our loved ones when they die. We typically put them in a nice casket with nice clothes. The ceremony is adorned with nice flowers, and loved ones and friends share many kind comments. This is as it should be. Still, the dead bodies are lowered into the ground and covered with dirt. Death—despite our efforts to camouflage it—is intrinsically dishonoring. After all, human beings were created to live forever with God, not to die and be buried in the ground.

In contrast to such dishonor, our new bodies will be glorious. They will never again be subject to aging, decay, or death. Never again will our bodies be buried in the ground. Our bodies will have awesome strength, energy, and abilities. We will never again have to lament, "I'm too tired." We'll be able to walk and jump with vitality. Our health and strength will never deteriorate or wane.

Finally, the apostle Paul affirms that our present mortal bodies are characterized by weakness, and he seems to be speaking from experience. Perhaps the older he got, the more this truth was confirmed in his own life. From the moment we are born, Paul says, our "outer self is wasting away" (2 Corinthians 4:16). Vitality decreases, illness comes, and old age follows with its wrinkles and decrepitude. Eventually, in old age, we may become utterly incapacitated, not able to move around and do the simplest of tasks. That's why nursing homes do such big business around the world.

By contrast, our body upgrades will be brimming with intrinsic power. We will never have to sleep in order to recoup energy. Never again will we tire, become weak, or become incapacitated.

All in all, words seem inadequate to describe the incredible differences between our present frail bodies and our future resurrection bodies. There will be no more cholesterol buildup, no more heart disease, no more kidney disease, no more diabetes, no more blindness or deafness, and no more aging of skin with wrinkles. We will enjoy perpetual youth with a fullness of vitality and energy.

Raised Physically

Scripture affirms that our resurrection bodies will be just like the resurrection body of Jesus Christ. The apostle Paul said that Christ "will transform our lowly body to be like his glorious body" (Philippians 3:21). John likewise said, "We know that when he appears we shall be like him" (1 John 3:2). This means that we will not be ethereal spirits floating around in a heavenly twilight zone for all eternity. Rather, we will be physically resurrected—just as Jesus was—and we will live in a physical place (see John 14:1-3).

How do we know Jesus was physically resurrected? The New Testament provides weighty evidence.

- Jesus's physical body was missing from the tomb (Matthew 28; Mark 16; Luke 24; John 20).
- Jesus's resurrection body retained the crucifixion scars (Luke 24:39; John 20:27).

- The resurrected Jesus affirmed He was not a spirit but rather had real flesh and bones (Luke 24:39).

- Jesus ate food in His resurrection body, thus proving the physicality of the resurrection (Luke 24:30,42-43; John 21:12-13).

- The resurrected Jesus was physically touched by others (Matthew 28:9; John 20:27-28; see also Luke 24:39-40).

- The word "body" (from the Greek word *soma*), used to describe the resurrection body in 1 Corinthians 15:44, always means a physical body in the New Testament when used of individual human beings.

Since our resurrection bodies will be like Jesus's resurrection body, we conclude that we will be physically resurrected. If this is true, however, what are we to make of 1 Corinthians 15:50, which states, "Flesh and blood cannot inherit the kingdom of God, nor does the perishable inherit the imperishable"?

At first glance, it might seem that this verse is arguing against the physicality of our resurrection bodies. But such is not the case. The phrase "flesh and blood" is a Jewish idiom that refers to mortal, perishable humanity. Mortal human beings in their present perishable bodies cannot inherit heaven. Mortal humanity must be made immortal humanity in order to survive in heaven. That's why 1 Corinthians 15:53 asserts that "this perishable body must put on the imperishable, and this mortal body must put on immortality." Put another way, the resurrection body will be endowed with special qualities that will enable it to adapt perfectly to life in God's presence.

Sturdy as a Building

We have seen that the apostle Paul compares our present earthly bodies to tents and our permanent resurrection bodies to buildings (2 Corinthians 5:1-4). Paul was speaking in terms his listeners would have understood. The Jews of Paul's day knew that the temporary tabernacle of Israel's wanderings in the wilderness was a giant tentlike structure. They also knew that it was eventually replaced with a permanent building—a stone temple—when Israel entered the promised land. Paul uses this contrast between the temporary tabernacle and the stone temple to represent the great contrast between our present bodies and our future resurrection bodies. The temporary "tent" (or body) in which believers now dwell will one day be replaced with an eternal, immortal, imperishable body (see 1 Corinthians 15:42,53-54).

When you think about it, we are constantly reminded in life that our temporal "tents" (or mortal bodies) are wearing out. Every time we look in the bathroom mirror—especially under a fluorescent lamp—we discover new signs of aging. Such reminders ought to direct our attention to the things of heaven, including our future body upgrades.

"Unclothed" for a Short Time

The day of resurrection—that is, the day of the rapture—is yet future. Until that day, our spirits depart the physical body and go to heaven at the moment of death. This can give us a sense of being "unclothed" for a short time. The apostle Paul talks about this in 2 Corinthians 5:4: "While we live in these earthly bodies, we groan and sigh, but it's not that we want to die and get rid of these bodies that clothe us. Rather, we want to put on our new bodies so that these dying bodies will be swallowed up by life" (NLT).

For Paul, being "unclothed"—that is, being without a physical body as a result of death—is a state of incompletion. For him, it carries a sense of nakedness. Even though departing to be with Christ in a disembodied state is far better than life on earth (Philippians 1:21), Paul's true yearning was to be clothed with a physically resurrected body (see 2 Corinthians 5:6-8). And that yearning will be fully satisfied on that future day of resurrection at the rapture. Paul himself was apparently hoping to take part in the rapture of the church, thereby escaping being unclothed for a time.

Meanwhile, Paul said, we groan (2 Corinthians 5:4). Why so? Because our bodies are burdened by sin, sickness, sorrow, and death. Our present bodies are so frail that we earnestly desire to have body upgrades that are free from all such suffering.

The Holy Spirit—a Guarantee

In 2 Corinthians 5:5, the apostle Paul affirmed that God has given us the Holy Spirit as a guarantee of what is to come in the afterlife. The word "guarantee," often translated "deposit," was typically used among the Greeks to refer to a pledge that guaranteed final possession of an item. It was sometimes used of an engagement ring, which guaranteed that the marriage would take place. The Holy Spirit's presence in our lives guarantees our eventual total transformation and glorification into the likeness of Christ's glorified resurrection body (see Philippians 3:21). The Holy Spirit in us is a pledge of what is to come.

This helps us to maintain an eternal perspective. It is true that our present bodies are wearing down. They've been infected by the fatal disease of sin. One day, they will simply cease functioning (they will fall down like a flimsy tent). By contrast, our resurrection bodies in heaven will never again wear down, never again get sick, and never again die. They will be as solid and sturdy as a building.

All this ultimately means that on that future day, God will defeat death once and for all. I love the way the apostle Paul puts it in 1 Corinthians 15:54-57.

> When the perishable puts on the imperishable, and the mortal puts on immortality, then shall come to pass the saying that is written: "Death is swallowed up in victory." "O death, where is your victory? O death, where is your sting?"…Thanks be to God, who gives us the victory through our Lord Jesus Christ.

Despair Replaced by Hope

Even people of God can lament the seeming shortness of earthly life. Job is a good example, for he was well familiar with the brevity and seeming futility of earthly life. "My days are swifter than a weaver's shuttle and come to their end without hope" (Job 7:6). "Man who is born of a woman is few of days and full of trouble. He comes out like a flower and withers; he flees like a shadow and continues not" (14:1-2).

If this short life were all we had to look forward to, we would have good reason to lament. As the apostle Paul put it so well, "If in Christ we have hope in this life only, we are of all people most to be pitied" (1 Corinthians 15:19). The good news, Paul goes on to say, is that our hope in Jesus extends far beyond the grave into life eternal. Just as Jesus was physically resurrected from the dead, so shall you and I be.

Paul said that Jesus's resurrection was the first of many to come: "Christ has been raised from the dead, the firstfruits of those who have fallen asleep" (1 Corinthians 15:20). Christ is the firstfruits in the sense that He was the first to be resurrected in His permanent resurrection body. The harvest—that is, the resurrection of you, me, and all other Christians—is yet to come. In fact, all who put their trust in Christ will be a part of that great harvest of resurrections from the dead. I can't wait!

> OUR FATHER, *thank You for sending Your Son into the world to die for us. Through His sacrifice, we are enabled and privileged to live and fellowship with You forever and ever. We are especially grateful that Jesus is the firstfruits of the resurrection and that we too will one day receive glorious resurrection bodies that will never grow old, get sick, or die. We are also thankful that You have given us the Holy Spirit as a guarantee of what is yet to come for us. You are an awesome God!*

6

Christians at the
Judgment Seat of Christ

I begin this chapter with a silly story that makes a powerful point.
John is the father of two sons—Matt and Ben. Matt comes home late in the afternoon and says to his father, "Dad, today was great. I was able to work down at the mission all morning, serving food to the homeless. In the afternoon, I was able to volunteer at the hospital, bringing comfort to the sick and dying."

John says to his son, "Well done, my son. Come on in to the kitchen and let me feed you a great meal."

Sometime later, Ben arrives home. He has the stench of alcohol on his breath. He boasts to his father, "Look at these music CDs—I stuffed them down my shirt and walked out of the music store. No one even noticed. What idiots! And as I was driving home, I'm pretty sure I hit someone on the road. I didn't stop though—I was in a hurry."

Then John says, "Well done, my son. Come on in to the kitchen, and I'll fix you a nice hot dinner."

I'm sure you would agree with me that such a story is absurd to the nth degree. The father in the story unjustly rewarded both sons equally despite the fact that one was righteous and the other was wicked. The story violates our sense of fairness.

This leads me to my main point. One day you and I will face the judgment seat of Christ. And Jesus, who is God, is perfectly just in His dealings with Christians.

Think about it. Some Christians are more holy and righteous than others. Some Christians are even carnal in their lifestyles. If God rewarded us all equally, regardless of our behavior, Jesus, the divine Judge, would be unjust.

The Bible has a lot to say about the justice of God (and Christ). That God is just means that He carries out His righteous standards justly and with equity. There is never any partiality or unfairness in His dealings with people (take a look at Genesis 18:25; Psalm 11:7; Zephaniah 3:5; John 17:25; Romans 3:26; Hebrews 6:10).

God is also all-knowing, which means that He is thoroughly acquainted with every detail of our lives—even the thoughts and emotions inside of us. Psalm 147:5 affirms that God's understanding is beyond measure. His knowledge is infinite (Psalms 33:13-15; 139:11-12; Proverbs 15:3; Isaiah 40:14; 46:10; Acts 15:18; 1 John 3:20; Hebrews 4:13). This means that when we are judged at the judgment seat, Christ, who is God, will not miss anything. His justice will be perfect.

God Rewards the Faithful

Both the Old and New Testaments are brimming with assurance that God rewards the faithful. Here is a small sampling of verses.

- "To you, O Lord, belongs steadfast love. You will render to a man according to his work" (Psalm 62:12).

- "One who sows righteousness gets a sure reward" (Proverbs 11:18).

- "The Lord GOD comes with might...behold, his reward is with him, and his recompense before him" (Isaiah 40:10).

- "Whatever good anyone does, this he will receive back from the Lord, whether he is a bondservant or is free" (Ephesians 6:8).

- "You have need of endurance, so that when you have done the will of God you may receive what is promised" (Hebrews 10:36).

- "Behold, I am coming soon, bringing my recompense with me, to repay everyone for what he has done" (Revelation 22:12).

The fact that God is a God of rewards is both an encouragement and a warning. It is an encouragement to those who are consistently serving Christ. It is a warning to those who have fallen into carnal living. God will render perfect justice in the end.

The Judgment Seat of Christ

The judgment seat of Christ is a prominent feature of the New Testament (see, for example, Romans 14:8-10; 1 Corinthians 3:11-15; 9:24-27; 2 Corinthians 5:10). On that sobering day, each Christian will give an account for all actions, words, thoughts, intentions, and motives of the heart. Christ will miss nothing.

The concept of a judgment seat has an interesting backdrop in New Testament times. It relates to the competitive sports of the day. After a sports contest ended, a dignitary sat on an elevated throne (Greek, *bema*) and dispensed rewards to the victors. Most often, the reward was a wreath of leaves, a symbol of victory. It was essentially a victor's crown. If he wore it in public, people would instantly surmise, "Ah, here is a winner of the contests." Christians will likewise stand before Christ, who will be seated on the *bema*, or judgment seat, and either receive rewards or suffer loss of rewards, depending on Christ's assessment.

I want to be careful to underscore that the judgment seat of Christ has nothing to do with whether Christ will save us and let us into heaven. In a number of Scripture verses, we are taught that once a person becomes a Christian, his or her salvation is secure, and nothing can threaten it or take it away (see, for example, John 10:28-30; Romans 8:29-39; Ephesians 1:13; 4:30; Hebrews 7:25). This judgment has only to do with the reception or loss of rewards for how one has lived after becoming a Christian. As one scholar notes, "Although those who have believed in Jesus have already been justified by faith (Rom. 5:1) and will not face condemnation on the final day (John 5:24; Rom. 8:1, 33), God will still judge their works (Rom. 14:10–12; 2 Cor. 5:10) and reward them accordingly (Matt. 6:1–6, 16, 18; 10:41–42)." [1]

Apparently, this judgment will take place immediately after the rapture. Once Christians enter into heaven, they will face the judgment seat of Christ. This theological inference is based on several scriptural facts. For example, many Bible expositors believe that the 24 elders in heaven represent believers (see Revelation 4:1,10). These elders have crowns on their heads at the very start of the tribulation period. If the elders represent believers, and if they already have crowns early in the tribulation period, we may logically surmise that they faced judgment right after the rapture.

Moreover, Scripture reveals that at the second coming of Christ, which follows the tribulation period, the bride of Christ (the corporate body of Christians) will return with Him. They will be adorned in "fine linen, bright and pure" (Revelation 19:8). Such apparel seems to indicate that believers have already passed through judgment. Again, then, Christians will face the judgment seat of Christ following the rapture, near the very beginning of the seven-year tribulation period.

Some May Experience Shame

One of the more sobering realities to ponder is that some Christians live a carnal lifestyle and may subsequently experience a sense of shame at the judgment seat of Christ. Such Christians will forfeit rewards that could have been theirs had they been faithful. This seems to be implied in 2 John 8, where John urges, "Watch yourselves, so that you may not lose what we have worked for, but may win a full reward" (see also 1 John 2:28). A loss of rewards is presented as a genuine possibility for the believer.

This does not mean that such a believer will live throughout the rest of eternity with profound regret and remorse. The fact that he remains saved and will live eternally in heaven in the presence of Christ will instill joy, even if he falls short at the judgment seat of Christ (see Psalm 16:11).

We Are Accountable for Our Actions

Are you up for a little self-examination? Consider these questions.

- God has given each of us certain talents. Do we consistently use them in His service?
- We have many opportunities throughout life to serve others. Do we consistently seize those opportunities to do good in His service?
- You and I face many temptations to do wrong. Do we typically give in, or do we resist temptation by the power of the Holy Spirit?

At the judgment seat of Christ, we will be accountable for all the actions we've done while in the body. The character of each Christian's life and service will be utterly laid bare under the unerring and omniscient vision of Jesus Christ, whose eyes are "like a flame of fire" (Revelation 1:14).

Both the Old and New Testaments point to our accountability for the actions we perform during earthly life. The psalmist affirms to the Lord, "You will render to a man according to his work" (Psalm 62:12). Christ "will repay each person according to what he has done" (Matthew 16:27). In Ephesians 6:8 we are told that "whatever good anyone does, this he will receive back from the Lord."

We Are Accountable for Our Thoughts

We are often skilled at hiding or masking our thoughts from other people. But none of us can hide our thoughts from God, who is all-knowing. Scripture reveals that our thoughts will be scrutinized at the judgment seat of Christ. God Himself affirms in Jeremiah 17:10, "I the LORD search the heart and test the mind, to give every man according to his ways, according to the fruit of his deeds." The apostle Paul later says something similar, affirming that God "will bring to light the things now hidden in darkness and will disclose the purposes of the heart. Then each one will receive his commendation from God"

(1 Corinthians 4:5). Jesus—who is Himself God—affirms, "I am he who searches mind and heart, and I will give to each of you according to your works" (Revelation 2:23).

We Are Accountable for Our Words

We can bring such blessing to others by our words, but we can also do incalculable damage with them (see James 3:1-12). It is hard to undo the damage done by our words once they've been uttered. As the old saying goes, once the toothpaste is out of the tube, it's hard to put it back in.

Scripture assures us that we'll be held accountable for our words at the judgment seat of Christ. In fact, in Matthew 12:36-37, Jesus Himself warned that "on the day of judgment people will give account for every careless word they speak, for by your words you will be justified, and by your words you will be condemned." No wonder Scripture often points to the wisdom of holding one's tongue and refraining from talk (Job 27:4; Psalm 39:1; Proverbs 13:3).

Our Accountability Embraces All of Life

We will be held accountable for how we govern our entire lives. I realize how scary this can be to ponder. But this realization serves as a strong motivator to live in a manner pleasing to the Lord.

- We will be held accountable for how we use our God-given talents and abilities (Matthew 25:14-29; Luke 19:11-26; 1 Corinthians 12:4-7; 2 Timothy 1:6; 1 Peter 4:10).

- We will be held accountable for how we spend our time (Psalm 90:9-12; Ephesians 5:15-16; Colossians 4:5; 1 Peter 1:17). (This is especially relevant to couch potatoes who park in front of the TV.)

- We will be held accountable for how we treat others (Matthew 10:41-42; Hebrews 6:10), show hospitality to strangers (Matthew 25:35-36; Luke 14:12-14), respond to mistreatment (Matthew 5:11-12; Mark 10:29-30; Luke

6:27-28,35; Romans 8:18; 2 Corinthians 4:17; 1 Peter 4:12-13), and endeavor to win souls for Christ (Proverbs 11:30; Daniel 12:3; 1 Thessalonians 2:19-20).

- We will also be held accountable for our attitude toward money (Matthew 6:1-4; 1 Timothy 6:17-19).

What Are the Rewards?

When Scripture speaks of the rewards we will either receive or lose at the judgment seat of Christ, it often refers to them as crowns. The various crowns mentioned in the New Testament relate to different kinds of Christian service and achievement.

- The crown of life is for Christians who persevere in the midst of trials—especially when they suffer to the point of death (James 1:12; Revelation 2:10).

- The crown of glory is given to Christians who faithfully and sacrificially minister God's Word to believers in the church (1 Peter 5:2-4).

- The crown incorruptible is bestowed on Christians who live by temperance and self-control (1 Corinthians 9:25).

- The crown of righteousness is awarded to Christians who yearn for the second coming of Christ (2 Timothy 4:8).

We would go awry if we were to conclude that these crowns are for our own glory. Ultimately these crowns are for the glory and honor of God. Indeed, in Revelation 4:10-11 we are told that believers will "cast their crowns before the throne, saying, 'Worthy are you, our Lord and God, to receive glory and honor and power, for you created all things, and by your will they existed and were created.'" This is in obvious keeping with the scriptural teaching that we were redeemed in order to bring glory to God (see 1 Corinthians 6:20).

In view of this, we can infer that in the afterlife, the greater the reward we receive, the greater will be our capacity to bring glory to God.

Conversely, we can infer that the lesser the reward we receive, the lesser will be our capacity to glorify God. We will have differing capacities to glorify God in heaven, all based on how we live our lives on earth. Is this not a powerful motivation for faithful service to the Lord?

That being said, I want to again emphasize that this does *not* mean some Christians will live throughout eternity with a sense of regret and remorse. After all, we'll all be saved, we'll all be living in heaven in the direct presence of Jesus Christ, and we'll all be glorifying God to the fullness of our capacity (see 1 Peter 2:9). As one of my colleagues often puts it, all of our cups will be running over, but some of our cups will be larger than others.

Build Your Life Well!

The apostle Paul teaches some important facts about the judgment seat of Christ in 1 Corinthians 3:11-15, especially regarding how we ought to build our lives.

> No one can lay a foundation other than that which is laid, which is Jesus Christ. Now if anyone builds on the foundation with gold, silver, precious stones, wood, hay, straw— each one's work will become manifest, for the Day will disclose it, because it will be revealed by fire, and the fire will test what sort of work each one has done. If the work that anyone has built on the foundation survives, he will receive a reward. If anyone's work is burned up, he will suffer loss, though he himself will be saved, but only as through fire.

If we build a life of effective God-glorifying service, we will be rewarded. If, however, we build a life of feeble spiritual commitment, we will suffer loss. All Christians will be saved, but not all will have equal reward. It is up to us to build our lives in a manner worthy of the Lord. We should live our lives in such a way that they have eternal value instead of wasting our lives on worthless endeavors.

I believe we ought to consider these words in 1 Corinthians 3:11-15 as a challenge rather than a threat. That is, consider it a challenge to joyfully live for Jesus, seek to obey Him, and hold on to those rewards. Don't go about daily living with a constant and oppressive legalistic mentality that God is like a cosmic Scrooge who is carefully eyeballing your every move with a view to getting even at the judgment. Never forget that God absolutely loves you and passionately wants to reward you. He's on your side! So let's reciprocate, showing our love for Him by living the way He wants us to. He'll reward us for it.

> OUR FATHER, *we revel in the reality that You are a God of perfect holiness, righteousness, justice, and truth. We are thankful that You never compromise with sin or evil. You are the perfectly righteous and just Judge of all the earth. We ask that the judgment seat of Christ would motivate each of us to live in a manner pleasing to You. Please empower us by the Holy Spirit to bear good fruit in our lives.*

7

New Heavens
and a New Earth

In the early 2000s, my family relocated from Southern California to Frisco, Texas, in order to be nearer our families. As soon as we drove into the neighborhood, our two kids—then young teenagers—saw the house at the end of the cul-de-sac and became giddy at the thought of seeing their new rooms in this brand-new house. As soon as we unlocked the front door, the kids darted up the stairs and inspected every square inch of their rooms, their closets, and the bathroom area. They couldn't have been more excited.

One day, we'll all have a similar feeling about the new heavens, the new earth, and our dwelling place in the New Jerusalem (the eternal city). We will no doubt remember our move-in day for the rest of all eternity.

Scripture reveals that the present heavens and earth will one day pass away. Why will God destroy the present earth and heavens? We find the answer in the Genesis account. In the Garden of Eden, Adam and Eve sinned against God, and God subsequently placed a curse on the earth (Genesis 3:17-18). Romans 8:20 tells us, "The creation was subjected to futility." Commenting on this verse, John MacArthur says that "decay, disease, pain, death, natural disaster, pollution, and all other forms of evil will never cease until the One who sent the curse removes it and creates a new heaven and a new earth (2 Pet. 3:13; Rev. 21:1)." [1]

Before God's eternal kingdom can be manifest, God must remove all vestiges of sin and darkness from the previous creation. A world permeated by sin and darkness will give way to a world infused with holiness and light. This is what will happen when God creates new heavens and a new earth.

Satan has long carried out his evil schemes on earth (see Ephesians 2:2). The earth must therefore be purged of all the stains of his extended presence. Satan will have no place in the new heavens and the new earth. All evidence of his influence will be removed when God destroys the earth and the heavens.

The destruction of the present heavens and earth is taught in both the Old and New Testaments. Psalm 102:25-26, for example, says of the passing of the old earth and heavens, "They will perish...they will all wear out like a garment...they will pass away." Isaiah 51:6 likewise affirms, "Lift up your eyes to the heavens, and look at the earth beneath; for the heavens vanish like smoke, the earth will wear out like a garment." Jesus was well aware of this common Old Testament teaching, for He contrasted the temporal universe with His eternal Word: "Heaven and earth will pass away, but my words will not pass away" (Matthew 24:35).

We receive a fuller revelation of the passing of the present heavens and earth in 2 Peter 3:7-13.

> The heavens and earth that now exist are stored up for fire, being kept until the day of judgment...The day of the Lord will come like a thief, and then the heavens will pass away with a roar, and the heavenly bodies will be burned up and dissolved, and the earth and the works that are done on it will be exposed.
>
> Since all these things are thus to be dissolved, what sort of people ought you to be in lives of holiness and godliness, waiting for and hastening the coming of the day of God, because of which the heavens will be set on fire and dissolved, and the heavenly bodies will melt as they burn! But according to his promise we are waiting for new heavens and a new earth in which righteousness dwells.

Commenting on this passage, one scholar notes that "the Old Testament consistently teaches that the cosmos is a moral universe created by God and that God will not let sin go unpunished forever. God is not only the creator of the universe; he is also the judge. The God who created the beginning of all things has the power to end them." [2] The good news is that although the present universe, which is stained by sin, will be judged and destroyed, God will create new heavens and a new earth for us to dwell in forever. And they will be glorious.

Which Heavens Become New?

If God will destroy the old heavens and create new heavens, one naturally wonders what heavens Scripture is referring to. Scripture actually refers to three different heavens. The first and second heavens are earth's atmosphere and the stellar universe (Genesis 1:17,20). The third heaven is God's domain—His perfect dwelling place (see Isaiah 63:15).

Scripture reveals that the only heavens that have been negatively affected by humankind's fall are the first and second heavens. The entire physical universe is running down and decaying. The third heaven—God's perfect and glorious dwelling place—remains untouched by human sin. It needs no renewal. This heaven subsists in moral and physical perfection and undergoes no change.

Once the physical universe is cleansed and God creates new heavens and a new earth, all vestiges of the original curse and Satan's presence will be utterly and forever removed. There will be a massive environmental change. We will instantly transition from an environment of pain, suffering, darkness, and death to a new environment of God-focused blessedness.

An Expansion of the Third Heaven

Many theologians believe that the term "heaven," presently used of God's perfect domain, will one day come to embrace and include the new heavens and the new earth. That means there will be a much wider meaning and a much larger territorial boundary for the third heaven. In other words, heaven will one day include the entire redeemed universe. We might say that heaven will include the entire *resurrected* universe.

This means that heaven and earth will no longer be separate realms, as they are now. They will be forever merged. Believers will thus continue to be in heaven even while they are on the new earth. The new earth will be utterly sinless, bathed and suffused in the light and splendor of God, which will not be obscured by evil or tarnished by evildoers.

So the third heaven that presently exists—the heaven believers now go to when they die (2 Corinthians 5:8; Philippians 1:21-23)—is different from the heaven that we will dwell in for all eternity after God creates the new heavens and new earth (2 Peter 3:13; Revelation 21:1). There's going to be a terrestrial and celestial renovation. God will one day merge His own domain of heaven with a newly renovated universe, and this newly renovated universe will be the eternal dwelling of believers of all ages. It will be perfect and glorious. In fact, the human brain is incapable of imagining the splendor of this new renovation (1 Corinthians 2:9).

In that day, the prophecy of Isaiah 65:17 will be fulfilled: "Behold, I create new heavens and a new earth, and the former things shall not be remembered or come into mind." Indeed, as Psalm 9:6 puts it, the wicked will come to an end, and the very memory of them will perish. This is what John describes in Revelation 21:1-5: "Then I saw a new heaven and a new earth, for the first heaven and the first earth had passed away…And he who was seated on the throne said, 'Behold, I am making all things new.'"

My brother or sister, we have cause to rejoice. We are destined for new heavens and a new earth!

The Nature of the "Newness"

Christians through the centuries have debated what Scripture means when it says the earth and heavens will be made new. Will God utterly annihilate the present universe and then create a brand-new universe? Or will He simply purify and renew the present universe? Highly respected Christians are on both sides of the debate.

Theologians call the first view the *replacement view*. This view holds that God will destroy our present universe and then create a new perfect and sinless universe. Advocates of this view like to cite Revelation

21:1,4, where we are told that "the first heaven and the first earth had passed away…the former things have passed away."

Other theologians counter that such phrases could easily apply to the *renewal view*. After all, Christians themselves are viewed as new creations, in which the old has passed away (2 Corinthians 5:17)—phrases that seem to point to their spiritual renewal, not their replacement. The renewal view thus states that the new heavens and new earth will be the present universe—but cleansed and purified of all evil, sin, suffering, and death. The new cosmos will stand in continuity with the present cosmos, but it will be utterly renewed and renovated. The universe will be transformed and perfected, purged of all that is not in keeping with eternal life.

Proponents of the replacement view rebut that 2 Peter 3:10-12 explicitly states that "the heavens will pass away with a roar, and the heavenly bodies will be burned up and dissolved…the heavens will be set on fire and dissolved, and the heavenly bodies will melt as they burn!"

Some scholars prefer to say that our present universe will be resurrected, just as our physical bodies will one day be resurrected. The idea here is that at the resurrection, we do not receive different bodies in place of our present bodies. Rather, our present bodies are resurrected so that there is a continuity between our earthly bodies and our resurrection bodies. It is suggested that the same will be true with the universe—it will be resurrected, thus having some continuity with the old heavens and earth. Just as our human bodies experience redemption, so the universe as a whole will experience redemption (see Isaiah 65:18-25; Ezekiel 28:25-26; 34:25-30; Matthew 19:28; Acts 3:21).

Randy Alcorn makes a great point in this regard. He suggests that we pay careful attention to the words we find throughout the Bible. "Reconcile. Redeem. Restore. Recover. Return. Renew. Regenerate. Resurrect. Each of these biblical words begins with the *re-* prefix, suggesting a return to an original condition that was ruined or lost." [3] Theologians suggest that just as many of Jesus's miracles involved restoration (such as restoration of health or even life), so God's renewal of the universe will involve restoration instead of replacement.

If this view is correct, perhaps the dissolving by fire mentioned in 2 Peter is a metaphorical reference to the renewal process, in which God removes the stain of evil and restores perfection. This is much like fire burning the dross out of iron.

Whether you hold to the replacement view or the renewal view, the important point is that our earth will one day be perfectly and wondrously adapted to the vast moral and physical changes that the eternal state necessitates. Everything will be new in the eternal state. Everything will be according to God's own glorious nature. The new heavens and the new earth will be brought into blessed conformity with all that God is—in a state of fixed bliss and absolute perfection.

Here is something to think about. Even our present earth has beautiful panoramas that stagger the aesthetic senses. Glorious sunrises defy description. On some days, the weather is so perfect that it feels Edenic outside. As wonderful as all this is, it dims in comparison to the glory of the coming new earth (1 Corinthians 2:9). I can't wait!

An Abundance of Christ's Glory

My friend, it gets even better! Scripture reveals that in the new heavens and the new earth, believers will share in the glory of Christ. Colossians 3:4 tells us, "When Christ who is your life appears, then you also will appear with him in glory" (see also Romans 8:17). This does not mean that you and I will become deity. However, like Christ, you and I will share in God's glory, with glorious resurrection bodies and shining robes of immortality, incorruption, and splendor. And we will live in a perfect, glorious environment. *Awesome!*

It Is Done!

In Revelation 21:6 God victoriously pronounces, "It is done!" This is a statement of divine finality. It represents a promise from God Almighty that what He has created for redeemed humanity's eternal state will indeed last forever and ever. Just as Jesus Himself uttered "It is finished" when He completed His redemptive work on the cross (John 19:30), so now God affirms that salvation for the redeemed of all ages has come to full fruition in the eternal state. All is now complete.

Never again will sin, Satan, or suffering surface among the redeemed. All is glorious.

> OUR FATHER, *You are the Creator of all things and are therefore worthy of worship. We are full of gratitude that one day, as the Creator, You will create new heavens and a new earth as our eternal habitat. We are grateful that all traces of sin and Satan will be removed, never again to injure us. We are thankful beyond words that one day we will have resurrection bodies and dwell in a resurrected universe. You are an awesome God!*

8

The New Jerusalem:
The Eternal City

God will one day create new heavens and a new earth. The entire universe will be renovated—indeed, resurrected. Scripture reveals that this new earth is where the New Jerusalem will be located. The New Jerusalem is the heavenly city where you and I will reside for all eternity (Revelation 21:10).

It is amazing to ponder that Jesus Christ is the actual builder of this city. We know this to be true because in John 14:2-3, Jesus addresses His fearful disciples with these words of comfort: "In my Father's house are many rooms. If it were not so, would I have told you that I go to prepare a place for you? And if I go and prepare a place for you, I will come again and will take you to myself, that where I am you may be also." Jesus is preparing our "place"—and that place, according to the book of Revelation, is the New Jerusalem, the eternal city of God and His children.

Jesus—a Wondrous Architect

I've often pondered the revelation that Jesus, the Builder of the eternal city, is the same one who designed and created the entire universe. How do we know Jesus created the universe?

Colossians 1:16 says of Jesus, "By him all things were created, in heaven and on earth, visible and invisible, whether thrones or dominions or rulers or authorities—all things were created through him and for him." John 1:3 likewise says of Jesus, "All things were made through him, and without him was not any thing made that was made" (see also Hebrews 1:2).

Jesus made it all—our solar system, our galaxy, and the other galaxies that are staggering distances from each other. It's an awesome thing to ponder.

When I was a child, one of my favorite pastimes was to go outside during the cold evenings in New Jersey, set up the family telescope (which we received for Christmas one year), and gaze into the stars for hours at a time. I loved it. I also remember visiting a planetarium, where we learned about the unfathomable distances between the stars and galaxies. The sheer immeasurable vastness of the universe staggered my relentlessly curious mind. Even today, I love to go outside at night and just stare at the stars. What a glorious universe the Lord Jesus has created!

If I might be so bold, however…you ain't seen nothin' yet! Christ is creating a splendorous place for us to dwell in for all eternity. The apostle Paul in 1 Corinthians 2:9 tells us that "no eye has seen, nor ear heard, nor the heart of man imagined, what God has prepared for those who love him." And Paul was speaking from experience, for he himself had been caught up to heaven, where he witnessed things firsthand (2 Corinthians 12:1-4).

The New Jerusalem—a Genuine City

Some people claim we can know little or nothing about what heaven is like. They say Scripture says very little about the topic, and what little it does say cannot be taken literally.

I have a much different view. As a longtime student of the Bible, I think Scripture tells us a great deal about heaven and the afterlife. Anyone who has eyes to see and ears to hear will find in the pages of Scripture an abundance of inspiring information about our wondrous destiny (see Isaiah 66:1; John 14:1-3; Acts 7:49; 2 Corinthians 12:2-4; Revelation 7:9; 22:1-5).

Perhaps the most elaborate description of the heavenly city (the New Jerusalem) is in Revelation 21:1-4.

Then I saw a new heaven and a new earth, for the first heaven and the first earth had passed away, and the sea was no more. And I saw the holy city, New Jerusalem, coming down out of heaven from God, prepared as a bride adorned for her husband. And I heard a loud voice from the throne saying, "Behold, the dwelling place of God is with man. He will dwell with them, and they will be his people, and God himself will be with them as their God. He will wipe away every tear from their eyes, and death shall be no more, neither shall there be mourning, nor crying, nor pain anymore, for the former things have passed away."

In this awe-inspiring passage, we are told that the New Jerusalem will come down out of heaven (where Jesus has constructed it) and will rest on the new earth. As this divine city comes down to the earth, we are assured that "the dwelling place of God is with man." Human beings and God will dwell together in the close confines of the New Jerusalem. We will dwell together!

I do not take references to this city to be symbolic of some kind of spiritual twilight zone where believers somehow float around in spiritual fellowship with God. Rather, I take the New Jerusalem to be a literal city, a real place where real resurrected people and a holy God will dwell together. A city has residences, means of transportation, government, bustling activity, various kinds of gatherings, and much more. There is no warrant for taking the descriptions of the New Jerusalem in Scripture as merely symbolic. Every description we have of the New Jerusalem in the Bible seems to imply a real place of residence.

This makes sense in view of the fact that you and I will have eternal and physical resurrection bodies (1 Corinthians 15:50-55). People with physical bodies must live in a physical place. And that physical place will be the New Jerusalem.

Splendorous in Every Way

The book of Revelation reveals some amazing facts about the New Jerusalem. It is so resplendently glorious that we have difficulty conceiving it and even more difficulty describing it. In the midst of this city are redeemed humans, celestial angels, and God Himself, who is identified as the Alpha and Omega, the beginning and the end. The Alpha and Omega affirms, "Behold, I am making all things new" (Revelation 21:5).

The city is made of resplendently glorious materials. The walls are built of jasper. The city itself is constructed with pure and shining gold that is "like clear glass" (Revelation 21:18). The streets, too, are made of gold that is transparent like glass (verse 21). This must be similar in some ways to the actual throne room of God, for "before the throne there was as it were a sea of glass, like crystal" (Revelation 4:6). Precious stones are everywhere. The gates are made of pearls.

The thing that is awesome to ponder is that this glorious city has no need of the sun or moon to shine, for the glory of God is its light. Keep in mind that the city is constructed of transparent gold with transparent streets and precious jewels scattered throughout. Imagine what it will be like as the divine glory shines throughout the city, reflecting and refracting everywhere.

The apostle John does a great job of describing the eternal city. Still, many theologians believe that although he was using the most beautiful terms he had access to, heaven is actually far more wondrous than human language can possibly capture. The actual experience of heaven will exceed anything the human mind can imagine (1 Corinthians 2:9). The description John gives may actually be but a faint shadow of the true reality, so glorious is the actual abode of heaven.

A Heavenly Habitat Void of Imperfections

In our present world, we are faced with imperfections of every kind. The environment is not perfect. Our health is not perfect. The food we eat is not perfect. Our relationships are not perfect. In fact, things are far from perfect in all these areas and more.

How different things will be in the eternal city. There will be no sin (and no sin nature in human beings), no curse, no influence from Satan or demons, no broken relationships, no hunger or thirst, no distance from God, no night or darkness, no fear, no pain or suffering, no tears, and no death. The very absence of such things seems impossible to imagine, but this is the reality that awaits each of us as believers.

The Biggest City Ever!

Revelation 21:16 reveals the gargantuan size of the New Jerusalem—12,000 stadia in length, width, and height. A stadia is 607 feet. This means that the length, width, and height of the New Jerusalem will be about 1400 miles. That's huge!

There is no good reason not to take this figure literally. After all, the eternal city must be large enough to accommodate the redeemed of all ages. Further, a large city is one that would be worthy of God.

A city this large would have a surface area of almost two million square miles. To give you a feel for how large this is, London is only 621 square miles. Quite obviously, earthly cities are dwarfed in comparison to the eternal city.

The New Jerusalem is 1400 miles high, so our highest skyscrapers are dwarfed in comparison. (The Empire State Building in New York City is 1454 feet high.) Because the New Jerusalem is so tall, it will likely have countless levels or stories. In fact, if a story is 12 feet high, the New Jerusalem could easily have 600,000 stories.

You may be wondering whether traveling throughout this city will be a formidable challenge. I don't think it will be. You and I will have resurrection bodies with amazing capabilities. These upgraded bodies will never get tired or grow weary. And besides, the city will be constructed of such awesomely beautiful materials that we'll marvel during every moment of travel.

Of course, it is impossible to say how many redeemed of the ages will actually be there. That is something only God Himself knows. But we do know that the New Jerusalem is big enough to accommodate a huge crowd. One mathematician calculated that if the New Jerusalem is shaped like a cube, it would have enough room for 20 billion residents if each individual residence were a massive 75 acres. There would also be plenty of room left over for parks and streets and other features that you'd likely see in any major city.

Some theologians believe that one argument in favor of the eternal city being a cube (as opposed to, for example, a pyramid) is that the Most Holy Place, God's dwelling place in Solomon's temple, was cube shaped (1 Kings 6:20). God Himself will dwell within the eternal city, so perhaps the New Jerusalem will be like a gigantic Most Holy Place. Of course, all this is speculation. We won't know the shape for sure until we actually inhabit the city on that future day.

High Walls but Open Gates

Scripture reveals that the New Jerusalem has "a great, high wall, with twelve gates, and at the gates twelve angels, and on the gates the names of the twelve tribes of the sons of Israel" (Revelation 21:12). Moreover, "the wall of the city had twelve foundations, and on them were the twelve names of the twelve apostles of the Lamb" (verse 14).

One could spend days pondering the significance of some of these facts. For example, why are the angels at the 12 gates? We know from other Scripture verses that angels have often functioned as guardians (Psalm 91:11; Matthew 18:10; Acts 12:15), so perhaps they are at the gates to guard the city. Angels in the Bible are also ministering (or serving) spirits (Hebrews 1:14). Perhaps they are at the gates as servants to those who inherit salvation.

Why are the names of the 12 tribes of Israel inscribed on the gates? It's hard to say. We might speculate it is because "salvation is from the Jews" (John 4:22), and the Messiah Himself came from Jewish lineage (Matthew 1:1).

Why are the names of the apostles inscribed on the foundations of the city? Again, it is hard to say. We might speculate that it is because the church itself was built upon the foundation of these men of God, who are therefore worthy of special honor (see Ephesians 2:20). John himself (the author of the book of Revelation) was one of those apostles. I wonder what his response might have been as he witnessed his own name inscribed on the foundations of the city. I suspect his response was one of great humility.

We might make another theological observation here. Scripture reveals that both Jews and Gentiles are a part of God's eternal family (Ephesians 2:11-13). It is therefore quite appropriate that the names of the 12 tribes of Israel and the 12 apostles be singled out in the eternal city.

When John describes the eternal city, he makes special mention of the fact that "its gates will never be shut by day—and there will be no night there" (Revelation 21:25). This is in obvious contrast to earthly cities of old. The nighttime was especially dangerous for earthly cities because invaders could approach by stealth and overcome the city while the people slept. Understandably, the gates of earthly cities of ancient times were always shut at night to help provide protection. In the New Jerusalem, however, there is no night, and the gates are always open. There will be no external threat from without, for Satan, demons, and unbelievers will be eternally quarantined in the lake of fire. And besides, God Himself will dwell within the eternal city. Who would dare attack it?

The River of the Water of Life

In Revelation 22:1-2 John says, "Then the angel showed me the river of the water of life, bright as crystal, flowing from the throne of God and of the Lamb through the middle of the street of the city." The biblical text does not reveal much about this river. Some have taken it to be merely symbolic, though others have taken it literally. Perhaps the best approach is to take it literally *and* symbolically. Perhaps this is a real and material river that symbolizes the rich abundance of the spiritual life of the redeemed in the eternal city. Just as a river provides a perpetual flow of thirst-quenching water on a sunny day, perhaps the river of the water of life symbolizes the ongoing provision of spiritual satisfaction and blessing to the redeemed, who are now basking in the warm glow of eternal life.

The Tree of Life

Revelation 22:2 then speaks of "the tree of life with its twelve kinds of fruit, yielding its fruit each month. The leaves of the tree were for the healing of the nations." The tree of life made its last appearance in the first book of the Bible—Genesis 3, where Adam and Eve are portrayed as having sinned against God. Paradise was lost, and the first couple were barred from access to the tree. Now, in the last book of the Bible, paradise is restored, and we again witness free access to the tree of life.

In what way do the leaves provide for the healing of nations? Does this imply that in the eternal state the nations will be in need of healing, as if recovering from some kind of conflict? I don't think so. After all, the state of affairs in the eternal state will be perfect and ideal in every way. Revelation 21:4 promises that in the eternal state "death shall be no more, neither shall there be mourning, nor crying nor pain anymore, for the former things have passed away."

It is noteworthy that the Greek word for "healing" in this verse is *therapeia*, from which the English word "therapy" is derived. The word carries the basic meaning of "health giving." In the present context, the word carries the idea that the leaves on the tree of life give health to the redeemed peoples of the world. They have nothing to do with correcting any ills, for such ills will not exist.

A Glorious Source of Light

We have seen that "the city has no need of sun or moon to shine on it, for the glory of God gives it light, and its lamp is the Lamb" (Revelation 21:23). This brings fulfillment to the prophecy in Isaiah 60:19: "The sun shall be no more your light by day, nor for brightness shall the moon give you light; but the LORD will be your everlasting light, and your God will be your glory."

We recall from the gospel of John that Jesus claimed, "I am the light of the world. Whoever follows me will not walk in darkness, but will have the light of life" (John 8:12). We also recall that Jesus once allowed His intrinsic divine glory to shine forth before some of His disciples. "He was transfigured before them, and his face shone like the sun, and his clothes became white as light" (Matthew 17:2).

The very light of God and of the Lamb of God will light up the eternal city forever. And because the light of God and the Lamb shine perpetually, there will never be night in the eternal city.

A City of Holiness

Revelation 21:2 describes the New Jerusalem as "the holy city." As

I once put it to a friend of mine, there will be no cops or lawyers in heaven, for holiness will predominate.

The truth is, there will be no sin or unrighteousness in heaven. Moral perfection will permeate the landscape. This does not mean you and I must attain moral perfection in order to enter heaven. Indeed, all who trust in Jesus Christ for salvation have been imputed with the very righteousness of Christ (see Romans 4:11,22-24). We have been made holy by Christ (Hebrews 10:14). We owe it all to Him!

> OUR FATHER, *we are so thankful for the wondrous future that lies ahead for each of us. We are in awe of the fact that Your plan of salvation, conceived in eternity past, will one day be brought into full fruition in the eternal state. Father, help us to remember that we are merely pilgrims en route to the final frontier of the New Jerusalem. We are just passing through this brief dot of time on earth. Help us not forget that we were not meant for this world alone, but are meant for heaven, our final home, our final destiny. Please empower us to resolve to spend our remaining time on earth wisely.*

9

No More Sin, Mourning, Pain, Tears, or Death

As I write, a number of my friends have terminal illnesses. One has cancer of the prostate gland. One has breast cancer. Another has pancreatic cancer and is presently in hospice care, awaiting his soon departure into heaven. Yet another has serious heart problems and could depart this life at any time.

Of course, these friends are doing everything medically possible to fight their illnesses and remain as healthy as possible. And many people are praying for each of them, asking for the Lord's healing intervention. Yet my friends are also aware of the survival statistics regarding their particular diseases. They are aware that God in His infinite wisdom does not always heal, and for reasons known only to Him, sometimes allows us to endure suffering and even die. Facing mortality can be a difficult thing.

And not only for those who are suffering the disease. In many cases, it is even more difficult for the family members and friends who remain on earth. Watching people deteriorate—seeing them daily become weaker and thinner and then die—can be a soul-draining experience. I've experienced it a number of times myself, as I suspect you have.

Each of us has an innate abhorrence of death and dying. After all, God created us to live. Life is a good thing. Death is an intrusive reality that first invaded our existence following Adam and Eve's sin against God. Death is an enemy! Death destroys life, in contrast to God, the Creator and author of life.

This built-in abhorrence of death is one thing that makes a focus on heaven so critically important. For in heaven, death and dying will be things of the distant past, never again to rear their ugly heads. In heaven, there will be only life, life, and more life.

Let us not forget, however, the grace shown in the deaths of Adam and Eve and all subsequent human beings. After all, death—as a judgment against sin—prevents human beings from living forever in a state of sin. When Adam and Eve sinned in the Garden of Eden (Genesis 2:17; 3:6), God assigned an angel to guard the tree of life. This was to protect Adam and Eve from eating the fruit of the tree of life while they were yet in bodies of sin. How horrible it would be to live eternally in such a state.

Through death, then, God graciously saw to it that every human being's existence in a state of sin had definite limits. And by sending a Savior into the world—the Lord Jesus Christ—God made salvation possible (Luke 2:11; John 3:17; 4:42; 1 Timothy 1:15). Those who believe in Him will live eternally at His side (John 3:15; 5:24).

Death Will Be Overcome

In Isaiah 25:8 we are told that God "will swallow up death forever; and the Lord God will wipe away tears from all faces." I like the Hebrew play on words in this verse. The ancient Jews often spoke of death as swallowing up the living, almost like a big mouth opening in the ground to devour people into the grave. But God promises that one day He will reverse things so that death itself will be swallowed up. When that happens, death will be gone forever.

The apostle Paul, himself an Old Testament scholar who was well aware of Isaiah 25:8, applied this truth to our future resurrection bodies. "When the perishable puts on the imperishable, and the mortal puts on immortality, then shall come to pass the saying that is written: 'Death is swallowed up in victory'" (1 Corinthians 15:54).

Also, just as Isaiah 25:8 promises that "the Lord God will wipe away tears from all faces," we read in Revelation 21:4 that God "will wipe away every tear from their eyes, and death shall be no more, neither shall there be mourning, nor crying, nor pain anymore, for the former things have passed away."

We're in for a big change. Those of us who watch the evening news on television receive regular reports of disaster, death, and mourning. But in heaven, all is life, life, and more life. We will never again be alerted to a sudden and deadly accident of a loved one or friend. No one will ever succumb to an incurable disease. We will never again attend a funeral service. There will be no more hearses. We will never again have to say a final farewell to anyone. We are headed for a glorious, deathless environment.

No More Mourning

Public mourning was a much bigger deal for the ancients than it is for us today. For that reason, the promise that in heaven there will be no more mourning would have caught their attention.

In modern times, mourning over someone's death is primarily an individual or family matter in which private tears are shed. But in Bible times, many people were involved in very visible and audible ways—and for an extended time. They showed their grief dramatically with loud weeping and wailing. As a sign of mourning, people put ashes on their heads, tore their clothing, walked barefoot, and shaved their beards off. (In modern days, a man shaving his beard off is no big deal. But in Bible times, almost all men had beards, so shaving let everyone know that a man was in mourning.)

One of the most bizarre aspects of mourning in Bible times is that families would often hire professional mourners. These people actually made a living by weeping and wailing at funerals. Once they were hired, they'd kick into high gear, and the grief-fest would begin.

In modern days, we do not set any time parameters for mourning. We mourn as long as we mourn, and that's that. But in Bible times, the traditional time of mourning was seven days. If the person who died was an important person, such as the patriarch of a family, the time of mourning might be longer. A person of high stature might be mourned for a very long time. For example, the beloved Joseph in the Old Testament was mourned for 70 days.

Though people mourn differently today than they did in Bible times, mourning will be with us as long as death continues to be with us. That means we will continue to mourn right up to the time when we enter heaven. Once there, we will never again experience mourning, for death will be gone forever.

In Revelation 21:4 we are assured that God "will wipe away every tear from their eyes, and death shall be no more, neither shall there be mourning, nor crying, nor pain anymore, for the former things have passed away." Likewise, Revelation 7:17 assures us that God "will wipe away every tear from their eyes."

Notice that both these verses use the phrase "every tear." This is an accurate translation from the Greek. God will not wipe away tears in some general sense, but rather every single tear, as if He pays special attention to each individual believer. I find this highly significant, for many, many things here on earth can bring tears to our eyes. But in heaven not a single tear will ever be found on our faces.

Having said this, I think it wise to make an important qualification. It is not as if in heaven, we'll have some cause to cry, after which the Lord immediately intervenes to resolve the issue so that tears are removed. No. Rather, what is communicated is that tears will be completely foreign to the heavenly experience. We will have nothing to cry about. In place of tears will be perpetual rejoicing. There will be no mourning, no crying, no pain, no suffering...ever!

Notice the transition that takes place from Genesis to Revelation. Death, tears, and mourning entered human existence in the first book of the Bible. These things resulted from Adam and Eve's rebellion against God. Death, tears, and mourning are then banished from human existence in the last book of the Bible. The effects of the curse will finally be removed. God will make all things new!

Will We Mourn Those Not in Heaven?

Through the years, I've been asked a number of times how we could possibly have no mourning in heaven while knowing that some family members and friends are not there with us. How could we not mourn, knowing that some are suffering in hell?

This is not an easy question to answer. I think part of the answer may be found in the fact that God may selectively purge some of our memories so that perhaps we do not think of anyone who might be in hell. I base this idea on Isaiah 65:17, which speaks of God's creation of new heavens and a new earth: "For behold, I create new heavens and a new earth, and the former things shall not be remembered or come into mind." The former things that shall not be remembered might include loved ones who rejected Christ and are now in hell. Such purging would be an act of grace and mercy on behalf of the saints in heaven.

I want to be careful to emphasize, however, that I do not think this verse means that God will purge every memory we have of the past. After all, many of our memories of the past are good memories—including the memory of how we became Christians and how we came to understand that Christ died for our sins. The fact that Christ's resurrection body retains the crucifixion scars will apparently serve as an eternal reminder of the sacrifice He had to pay for our salvation (John 20:27). As well, we will continue many of our present relationships in heaven, so it makes good sense that we would retain precious memories about those relationships (consider Luke 16:19-31).

In addition to the fact that God may selectively purge some memories, we must also remember that God has promised that He will take away all pain and remove all our tears (Revelation 21:4). It is in His hands. It is His responsibility. We may not be fully aware of how God will do it, but we can rest assured that He has the power and ability to do as He has promised. It is a concrete fact that we will be serenely happy in heaven. God has promised it, and He will bring it about.

More generally, in the heavenly state we will each be aware of the full justice of all of God's decisions. We will clearly see that those who are in hell are there precisely because they rejected God's only provision for escaping hell, choosing instead the path of sin, suffering, and death.

We will see things clearly from the divine perspective. We will see that God's divine love does not coerce people against their wills into the kingdom of God. God invites all, but many reject the invitation. Those who reject the invitation are eternally quarantined from heaven, and all in heaven will fully understand God's perfect justice in this quarantine.

Each of us will also see God's perfect justice in the various degrees of punishment among those consigned to hell (Matthew 10:15; 16:27;

Luke 12:47-48). This assures us that the Hitlers of human history will suffer much more than, for example, a non-Christian moralist. God is perfectly wise and just. He knows what He is doing! You and I can rest with quiet assurance in God's wisdom and justice when it comes to judging unbelievers.

Ultimately, we have to take God at His Word. He has promised there will be no more mourning, pain, or tears in heaven. He will bring it about.

Keeping Things in Perspective

Life on earth is full of pain, suffering, disease, and death. Life in heaven will be absent of all these things. Let's also keep in mind that life on earth is short, but life in heaven is long. This ought to put wind in our spiritual sails during earthly doldrums. We read in 1 Peter 1:6-7, "There is wonderful joy ahead, even though you have to endure many trials for a little while. These trials will show that your faith is genuine. It is being tested as fire tests and purifies gold—though your faith is far more precious than mere gold. So when your faith remains strong through many trials, it will bring you much praise and glory and honor on the day when Jesus Christ is revealed to the whole world" (NLT).

> OUR FATHER, *in a world of suffering and pain, we are thankful for the promise of a future that will have no such suffering and pain. In a world of pervasive death, we are thankful for the promise of a future that will have no death. As we live day to day, we ask that You help us keep things in perspective and enable us to see that even in our present suffering, You are working in our lives to bring about good. We praise You for Your work in our lives—even when it hurts a little.*

10

Satan and Demons
Eternally Quarantined

Living the Christian life today is difficult. One reason for this is that we each have a sin nature within us, which means we have a bent toward committing evil acts. We also live in a world that offers many enticements to engage in evil. Still worse, we live in an environment infested with evil spirits who not only are the archenemies of God but also seek to attack any person who is committed to Christ.

With this in mind, I want you to consider the implications of our relocation to heaven. Obviously, unlike the world, heaven will provide no enticements to sin. You and I as Christians will no longer have a sin nature in our resurrection bodies. And Satan will be eternally quarantined away from us in the lake of fire. In this chapter, I will demonstrate that Satan's eternal banishment is profoundly important to the happiness of the saints in heaven.

The Big Picture of Satan's Banishment

In Revelation 20:10, the apostle John describes Satan's banishment. "The devil who had deceived them was thrown into the lake of fire and sulfur where the beast and the false prophet were, and they will be tormented day and night forever and ever." Notice three primary factors here:

1. The place of confinement is the lake of fire—a synonym for hell.

2. The duration of confinement is "day and night forever and ever."

3. The punishment in this confinement is torment.

Let us be clear that Satan will never be released from the lake of fire. He is consigned to hell without possibility of redemption or release. After we've been in heaven with Christ for 100 billion years, Satan will still be confined in the lake of fire, and there he will forever remain.

This is one of the factors that adds significance to Revelation 21:25, which tells us that the gates of the New Jerusalem—the eternal city of the redeemed that will rest on the new earth—will never be shut. Those who dwell in the eternal city will never have any external threat. Satan, demons, and unbelievers will be in eternal quarantine in hell with no possibility of escape.

This also adds significance to the peace, serene rest, and joy that the redeemed will enjoy in heaven (Revelation 14:13). After all, how could the redeemed enjoy peace, serene rest, and joy in the midst of constant temptations and afflictions from Satan and demons? It wouldn't be possible. But with Satan and demons out of the picture forever, and with sin completely absent, peace, serene rest, and joy become realities. Gone forever will be Satan's temptations toward evil. Gone forever will be his attempts to afflict us with bodily ailments. Gone forever will be the seeds of doubt he seeks to sow in our minds.

Still further, Satan's banishment to the lake of fire helps us to understand the significance of God creating new heavens and a new earth. Satan and demons have long worked on this earth to bring about the downfall of God's people and lure them into sin. The stench of their presence is found throughout the creation (see Ephesians 2:2). This means that God must purge the present earth and the present heavens (earth's atmosphere and stellar space) of all the stains resulting from their extended presence. God will create new heavens and a new earth that will be purified from their contamination.

The Details of Satan's Banishment

Now that we understand the big picture of Satan's banishment, let's zero in on some of the details. These details will give us enhanced appreciation for our wondrous experience in heaven.

1. Satan's present influence is immense. Scripture describes him as being extremely powerful and influential in the world. He is called "the god of this world" (2 Corinthians 4:4). This does not mean Satan is deity. It simply means that this is an evil age, and Satan is its god in the sense that he is the head of it. Also, as god of this world, Satan is the promoter of all cults and false religions that stand against the truth of Christianity.

Satan is also called the "ruler of this world" (John 12:31). The key word here is "world." This word refers not to the physical earth but to an anti-God system that Satan has promoted. It conforms to his ideals, aims, and methods. He is the head of this evil system.

Satan is further called the "prince of the power of the air" (Ephesians 2:2). In this context, the air seems to be the sphere in which the inhabitants of this world live. This sphere represents the very seat of Satan's authority. Satan is portrayed as having power in the governmental realm (Matthew 4:8-9; 2 Corinthians 4:4), the physical realm (Luke 13:11,16; Acts 10:38), the angelic realm (Jude 9; Ephesians 6:11-12), and the religious realm (Revelation 2:9; 3:9).

In view of this, just ponder for a few moments the significance of this formerly massive evil influence being utterly absent in the heavenly estate. No longer will he be the "ruler of this world" or "the god of this world." No longer will he exercise power in the governmental, physical, angelic, and religious realms. I cannot even begin to capture in words the blessing of Satan's complete absence from heaven.

2. Satan is presently "the accuser of our brothers" (Revelation 12:10). The Greek tense used in Revelation 12:10 reveals that accusing Christians is Satan's continuous, ongoing work. He never lets up. Theologians believe Satan engages in two primary activities in this regard. He continually brings charges against believers before God (see Zechariah 3:1), and he continually accuses believers to their own consciences, making them feel perpetual shame and guilt. Just think of how wonderful it will be in heaven to never have to endure such accusations again.

3. Satan presently promotes filth. In Matthew 12:24 the Pharisees refer to Satan as Beelzebul. This word literally means "lord of the flies" and carries the idea, "lord of filth." The devil corrupts everything he touches. He promotes filthy living and immorality. Satan is also called the evil one (1 John 5:19). He opposes all that is good and promotes all that is evil. Indeed, he is the very embodiment of evil. What a blessing it will be in heaven to have this promoter of evil forever banished.

4. Satan presently stands against us as we seek to serve God. Scripture refers to Satan as our adversary (1 Peter 5:8). This word indicates that Satan opposes us and stands against us in every way he can. Satan is also called the devil (Matthew 4:1), a word that also means "adversary." The devil was and is the adversary of Christ, so he is also the adversary of all who seek to follow Christ. In heaven, however, Satan will no longer be around to be our adversary. We'll be able to serve and worship the Lord without hindrance.

5. Satan is presently a promoter of lies. He is called the father of lies in John 8:44. The word "father" is used in this verse metaphorically of the originator of a family or company of persons animated by a deceitful character. Satan was the first and greatest liar. Heaven will be permeated by truth because Satan will be forever absent.

6. Satan presently tempts believers to sin. Satan is called the tempter in Matthew 4:3. His constant purpose is to incite human beings to sin. He whispers the most plausible excuses and enticing reasons to sin against God. This will no longer be the case in heaven, for Satan will not be there. And besides, you and I will no longer have a sin nature with a bent toward evil. It will be wonderful!

Related to this, Satan is also called a serpent (Genesis 3:1; Revelation 12:9). The serpent is characterized by treachery, deceit, venom, and murder. He tempts believers to sin, knowing that sin leads to death. In heaven, however, believers will have neither temptations nor sin, and death will be a thing of the distant past.

7. Satan presently harasses and attacks Christians in various ways. Scripture reveals that Satan tempts believers to lie (Acts 5:3) and to commit sexually immoral acts (1 Corinthians 7:5). Satan hinders the work of believers in any way he can (1 Thessalonians 2:18) and causes

division among them (Matthew 13:38-39). He incites persecutions against believers (Revelation 2:10). He plants doubt in the minds of believers (Genesis 3:1-5), fosters spiritual pride in their hearts (1 Timothy 3:6), and leads them away from "a sincere and pure devotion to Christ" (2 Corinthians 11:3). Such things will be completely absent in heaven, for Satan will be quarantined in the lake of fire.

8. Satan is a murderer. Satan is called a murderer in John 8:44. Hatred is the motive that leads one to commit murder, and Satan hates both God and His children. "Murder" won't even be in the vocabulary of heaven! The chief murderer will be forever quarantined in the lake of fire.

9. Satan presently seeks to destroy us. In 1 Peter 5:8 we are told that the devil "prowls around like a roaring lion, seeking someone to devour." This graphic simile depicts Satan's strength and destructiveness. In heaven, however, there is no fear of such destruction, for Satan is quarantined, and the Lord reigns in strength.

10. Satan is presently a counterfeiter of the one true God and His divine program. Satan has long desired to take the place of God. He mimics God in many ways. This is hinted at in 2 Corinthians 11:14, which refers to Satan masquerading as an angel of light.

Consider some of the ways that Satan has sought to mimic God:

- Satan has his own church—the "synagogue of Satan" (Revelation 2:9).

- He has his own ministers of darkness who bring false sermons (2 Corinthians 11:4-5).

- He has formulated his own system of theology, sometimes called "doctrines of demons" or "teachings of demons" (1 Timothy 4:1; see also Revelation 2:24).

- His ministers proclaim his gospel, which Paul calls "a gospel contrary to the one we preached to you" (Galatians 1:7-8).

- Satan has his own throne (Revelation 13:2) and his own worshippers (verse 4).

- He inspires false Christs (Matthew 24:4-5).

- He employs false teachers who bring in "destructive heresies" (2 Peter 2:1).

- He sends out false prophets (Matthew 24:11).

- He sponsors false apostles who imitate the true (2 Corinthians 11:13).

In heaven, such deception will nowhere be seen. Only truth will permeate the eternal kingdom of heaven. Jesus Christ, who is the truth (John 14:6), will reign in the kingdom of truth (heaven).

11. Satan tries to thwart Christ in any way he can. Scripture reveals that Satan has long had a dark agenda in trying to thwart the person and mission of Jesus Christ.

- Matthew 2 reveals that Joseph, Mary, and Jesus had to flee to Egypt, having been warned by an angel that Herod sought to murder Christ (verses 13-16). The account in Matthew does not mention the involvement of Satan, but Revelation 12:4-6 makes it clear that Satan was behind the murderous intent.

- Following His baptism, Jesus was led into the wilderness, where He was tempted by the devil for 40 days (Matthew 4:1-11). Of course, Christ as God could not be made to sin. But Satan still made the attempt in hopes of disqualifying Christ from being the Savior.

- During some of Jesus's encounters with Israel's religious leaders, He saw the work of Satan in their actions. For example, some of the Jewish leaders sought to have Jesus put to death. Jesus responded, "You are of your father the devil, and your will is to do your father's desires. He was a murderer from the beginning" (John 8:44).

- Jesus also saw the work of Satan among those He was closest to. When Jesus predicted His own death, Peter rebuked Him and said, "Far be it from you, Lord! This shall never happen to you" (Matthew 16:22). Jesus then said to Peter, "Get behind me, Satan! You are a hindrance to me" (verse 23). Jesus recognized, in Peter's words, Satan's attempt to stop Him from going to the cross.

These and other verses indicate that the devil did everything he could to thwart the mission of Jesus Christ. In heaven, Christ will have no such hindrance. How wondrous it will be for sinless, redeemed humanity to dwell with Christ, unhindered in any way by the evil one. What sweet fellowship awaits us.

12. In keeping with the above, no longer will Christians be attacked or harassed by demons—evil spirits who follow the lead of Satan. Scripture reveals that demons, who are also called fallen angels, seek to harm Christians in many ways.

- Demons hinder answers to the prayers of believers (Daniel 10:12-20).

- Demons endeavor to instigate jealousy and create factions among believers (James 3:13-16).

- Demons would separate believers from Christ if they could (Romans 8:38-39).

- Demons cooperate with Satan in working against believers (Matthew 25:41; Ephesians 6:12; Revelation 12:7-12).

There will be no such demonic affliction in heaven, for demons will be quarantined in hell along with their leader, Satan.

Free at Last!

I am sure you now understand what I mean when I say that Satan's banishment to the lake of fire has profound implications for our life in heaven. Heaven involves not just the presence of all that is blessed but also the complete absence of all that harms. I can't wait!

OUR FATHER, *we are thankful that even today You have made provisions for us to be protected from the evil one. But we are profoundly grateful that when we're in heaven, Satan and demons will be eternally quarantined away from us forever. You have arranged a glorious destiny for us, removing all that is hurtful and blessing us with all that is good. For this we praise You and thank You. You are truly an awesome God!*

11

Earthly Realities
Absent in Heaven

We're all used to the way things are here on earth. Most of us have routine days. But many of the things we're accustomed to on earth will simply not be in heaven. In like manner, many of the things we typically do on earth will never happen in heaven. Let's briefly consider some of these things to enhance our understanding of what happens after life.

No Physical Temple

Scripture reveals that there is no physical temple that one must enter to encounter God's presence in heaven. In fact, we are told that God Himself is the temple for believers in heaven. In Revelation 21:22, the apostle John affirms, "I saw no temple in the city, for its temple is the Lord God the Almighty and the Lamb."

The term "temple" is used in quite a number of different ways in the Bible. In Old Testament times, the term referred to the holy building where God's presence was made known to the people. In New Testament times, the temple was not a building but was rather the people of God. We read in 1 Corinthians 3:16, "Do you not know that you are God's temple and that God's Spirit dwells in you?"

John did not see a physical temple in the eternal city because God Almighty and the Lamb (Jesus Christ) are its temple. Most Bible expositors take this to mean that in the New Jerusalem, God's presence will not be limited to a single building within the city. Rather, His presence will permeate the entire city. References to serving God within His temple (Revelation 3:12; 7:15) would thus seem to point to believers serving God in His very presence.

Another point bears mentioning here. In a previous chapter I noted that the eternal city (the New Jerusalem) is 1400 miles long, 1400 miles wide, and 1400 miles high. Many theologians believe this city will be cubical, much like the Most Holy Place was in the Old Testament temple. It is possible that the New Jerusalem is intended to reflect the shape of the Most Holy Place, only much larger. This being so, there is no need for a separate temple, for indeed, all is already holy within the city. There will be no antithesis of sacred and secular in heaven.

No Night and No Need of the Sun

Revelation 22:5 tells us that in the eternal city, "night will be no more. They will need no light of lamp or sun, for the Lord God will be their light." There are two observations I want to make for you.

First, our present bodies are comparatively weak and need sleep every night in order to recuperate. Our resurrection bodies will apparently not require recuperation through sleep. Our upgraded bodies will never become fatigued. We will never become run-down. Therefore, night becomes entirely unnecessary.

Second, the fact that the glory of the Lord God will light up the eternal city may have a parallel to the Old Testament tabernacle, and later, the temple. Recall that when the tabernacle in the wilderness was completed, the cloud of the Lord's glory settled upon it, preventing human entrance. "The cloud covered the tent of meeting, and the glory of the LORD filled the tabernacle. And Moses was not able to enter the tent of meeting because the cloud settled on it, and the glory of the LORD filled the tabernacle" (Exodus 40:34-35).

Likewise, the cloud of the Lord's glory filled Solomon's temple when it was dedicated. "When the priests came out of the Holy Place, a cloud filled the house of the LORD, so that the priests could not stand to minister because of the cloud, for the glory of the LORD filled the house of the LORD" (1 Kings 8:10-11).

Here is my point. Just as the glory of the Lord filled (and lit up)

Solomon's temple, so the glory of the Lord will fill and light up the eternal city, the New Jerusalem, itself possibly modeled after the Most Holy Place in the temple. But there is one notable difference. In Old Testament times, the glory of the Lord prevented human entrance into the temple. By contrast, Christians, in their upgraded resurrection bodies, will be perfectly comfortable in the New Jerusalem as they bask in the warm glow of the Lord's glory. Our resurrection bodies will be specially suited to dwelling in the direct presence of the Lord Almighty.

No Sea

About three-quarters of the earth's surface is presently covered with water and is therefore uninhabitable. In the new earth, by contrast, there will be no sea (Revelation 21:1). This means there will be an immensely increased land surface, making the whole world inhabitable. The life principle in this new earth will not be water but rather "the water of life" (22:1).

Bible expositors observe that for some people, the sea calls to mind the great destructive flood of Noah's time. As well, for many people, the sea constitutes a barrier between loved ones, who may live on opposite sides of the ocean. Keep in mind that as the apostle John wrote the book of Revelation, he was exiled on the island of Patmos, surrounded by water on every side and thereby prevented from contact with his loved ones throughout Asia Minor. There will be no sense of separation on the new earth. Fellowship will never be broken!

No More Curse

Revelation 22:3 tells us, "No longer will there be anything accursed, but the throne of God and of the Lamb will be in it, and his servants will worship him." Following humanity's fall in the Garden of Eden, a curse was placed on the earth by God. "Cursed is the ground because of you; in pain you shall eat of it all the days of your life; thorns and thistles it shall bring forth for you; and you shall eat the plants of the field" (Genesis 3:17-18). Romans 8:20 thus reveals that "the creation was subjected to futility."

Before the eternal kingdom of heaven can be made manifest, God must deal with this cursed earth. When God creates new heavens and a new earth, the curse will finally be removed. The bad will give way to the good. The negative will give way to the positive. Darkness will give way to the light. All will be made new (Revelation 21:5).

No More Pain, Death, Mourning, or Satan

There will be no further pain, death, mourning, or Satan in heaven (see Revelation 21:4). There will be no more suffering—physical, emotional, spiritual, or any other. The "last enemy" (death) will be forever gone, never again to surface among the living (1 Corinthians 15:26,54-55). Mourning will therefore not even be in heaven's vocabulary. And, as we have seen, Satan and demons will be eternally quarantined in the lake of fire, never again to harass the saints of God (Revelation 20:10).

Things We Won't Experience in Heaven

In heaven we will have resurrection bodies with no sin nature. Satan and demons will be eternally quarantined away from our presence forever. And we will live in a perfectly holy environment. As a natural consequence of this wondrous state of affairs, many things will be foreign to our experience in heaven. The following is just a sampling.

- We will never have to confess a wrongdoing. With no sin in heaven, confession will be unnecessary.

- We will never experience guilt or shame over any action.

- We will never have to repair our homes or any other items. Nothing will run down.

- We will never have to defend ourselves before others. Relationships will be perfect in every way.

- We will never have to apologize. Our actions will be focused on others instead of ourselves.

- We will never feel isolated or lonely. There will be a perfect expression of love between all the redeemed.

- We will never have to go through rehabilitation. We will remain whole and healthy for all eternity. There will never be any addictions of any kind.

- We will never be depressed or discouraged. We will perpetually enjoy the abundant life.

- We will never become tired or worn-out in heaven. Our resurrection bodies will be strong and never need recuperation.

- There will never be offense (given or received) in heaven. All our words will be void of sin and full of grace.

- We will never experience envy or jealousy in heaven. Our love for others will be utterly complete and perfect, with no unwholesome emotions.

- We will never experience infidelity in heaven. The Golden Rule will unwaveringly predominate. Faithfulness will be a hallmark of heaven.

- We will never again lust after another person. Our hearts will be pure, with no sin whatsoever.

- We will never experience a misunderstanding with other people. No relationships will ever be broken.

- We will never have any sense of deprivation. We will never have to earn money or worry about having enough money to survive. We'll have an overabundance of all we need.

- There will be no wars or bloodshed in heaven. The sinful attitudes that give rise to wars will be nonexistent.

Of course, there are many other things I could mention here. The main point I want to stress is that the absence of all these (and many other) negative things will contribute immensely to our sense of joy and well-being in heaven. We can't even begin to imagine how wonderful it will be.

Contrasting the Eternal City with Earthly Cities

In view of what will and will not be in heaven, there is a noted contrast between the New Jerusalem and earthly cities. Here is just a sampling.

- Earthly cities constantly have to be rebuilt or repaired, but no such repair is ever necessary in the New Jerusalem.

- Believers and unbelievers live in earthly cities, but only believers will be in the eternal city.

- Many people go hungry and thirsty in earthly cities, but no one will hunger or thirst in the New Jerusalem.

- Earthly cities have crime, but there is perfect righteousness in the eternal city.

- Earthly cities often have outbreaks of rebellion, but there is no such rebellion in the heavenly city. All are in submission to the divine King, Jesus Christ.

- People in earthly cities have many broken relationships, but all relationships in the New Jerusalem are perfect and loving.

- Widespread disease is common in earthly cities, but perfect health predominates in the New Jerusalem.

- Earthly cities have graveyards, but such are absent in the eternal city. Death will be entirely foreign to our experience in heaven.

- Earthly cities get dark at night, but the eternal city is always lighted.

Again, I could obviously draw many other contrasts here. But the point is obvious. Our existence in heaven will be completely unlike our experience on earth. The eternal city, the New Jerusalem, is going to be absolutely wonderful, far more so than any human mind could possibly fathom or even begin to imagine. As 1 Corinthians 2:9 puts it, we will experience on a moment-by-moment basis "what no eye has seen, nor ear heard, nor the heart of man imagined."

OUR FATHER, *You are an all-wise God. You know what is best for us. You have designed heaven to be a place of optimal blessing for us. You have decreed what will be there and what will not be there. We praise You for the love You have expressed to us in providing so great a salvation. What an awesome joy it will be to fellowship with You for all eternity.*

12

Face-to-Face
Fellowship with God

Fellowship with God. It is the cry of the human heart, the yearning of the soul. The psalmist cried out, "As a deer pants for flowing streams, so pants my soul for you, O God. My soul thirsts for God, for the living God. When shall I come and appear before God?" (Psalm 42:1-2). Likewise, in Psalm 63:1, the psalmist yearned, "O God, you are my God; earnestly I seek you; my soul thirsts for you; my flesh faints for you, as in a dry and weary land where there is no water."

Throughout human history, God has fellowshipped with His people in various ways. How exciting it must have been for the patriarchs—men like Abraham, Isaac, and Jacob—to see God appear in the form of the "angel of the LORD" (see Genesis 22:11-15). He appeared to Moses in a burning bush and conversed with him (Exodus 3:2). When God delivered His people from enslavement in Egypt, He led them in the wilderness in the form of a pillar of cloud during the daytime hours and a pillar of fire during the night (Exodus 13:21-22).

In New Testament times, God directly dwelt among His people in the person of Jesus Christ (John 1:1,14,18). Jesus, though fully God as the second person of the Trinity, took on human flesh so that in the incarnation, He was 100 percent God and 100 percent man (see Philippians 2:5-11). This is why Jesus could say to His followers, "Whoever has seen me has seen the Father" (John 14:9).

In modern times, God makes Himself present to us through the Holy Spirit (see John 14–16). Indeed, every Christian is a temple of the

Holy Spirit (see 1 Corinthians 3:16; 6:19). God the Holy Spirit dwells in every Christian every bit as much as God dwelt in the temple in Old Testament times (for example, see Ezekiel 10:4).

God has clearly appeared to and interacted with humans throughout the centuries in various ways. And He has always been the aggressor in making Himself known to people.

In the future, it only gets better! On a future day, when we finally enter the eternal state in heaven, we will have unhindered, full access to God and will behold Him face to face. The apostle John declared that God's people "will see his face" (Revelation 22:4). The apostle Paul likewise exulted, "Now we see in a mirror dimly, but then face to face. Now I know in part; then I shall know fully, even as I have been fully known" (1 Corinthians 13:12). Such verses bring to mind the declaration of the psalmist: "As for me, I shall behold your face" (Psalm 17:15).

Often when people think of heaven, they ponder the reality that they will live forever and that death will be finally defeated. As wondrous as this is, the true wonder of heaven lies in the reality that we will fellowship with God face to face. Just think about it. Can anything be more sublime and more utterly satisfying for the Christian than to enjoy the sheer delight of unbroken fellowship with God and to have immediate and completely unobstructed access to the divine glory? (See John 14:3; 2 Corinthians 5:6-8; Philippians 1:23; 1 Thessalonians 4:17.) The human mind can scarcely take all this in. We will actually gaze upon the countenance of eternal God!

Surely there can be no greater joy or exhilarating thrill for the creature than to look upon the face of the divine Creator and fellowship with Him forever. Our eternal God—the One "who alone has immortality, who dwells in unapproachable light" (1 Timothy 6:16)—will dwell intimately among His people. As the book of Revelation puts it, "They will be his people, and God himself will be with them as their God" (Revelation 21:3). And as the psalmist so eloquently exclaimed, "In your presence there is fullness of joy; at your right hand are pleasures forevermore" (Psalm 16:11).

No longer will our fellowship with God be interrupted by sin and defeat. Our communion with Him will be continuous and unbroken, for sin will no longer be among us. All things will be made new.

To fellowship with God will be the essence of heavenly life, the fount and source of all blessing. The crowning wonder of our experience in the eternal city will be the perpetual and endless exploration of the unutterable beauty, majesty, love, holiness, power, joy, and grace of God Himself.

When I ponder such wondrous heavenly realities, I sometimes reflect back to the gospel of Matthew, where we are informed that one of Jesus's names is Immanuel, which means "God with us" (Matthew 1:23). We all ought to meditate on the reality that in the eternal state, Jesus as God will be with us in the closest possible sense.

Death Means Direct Fellowship

While we are living on earth, we can fellowship with God spiritually. But at death, our spirits depart the physical body and are ushered directly into heaven, where our direct and unhindered fellowship with God begins.

There are many scriptural evidences for this wondrous reality. Consider, for example, the thief on the cross who expressed faith in Christ. Christ—also on the cross—indicated to him that he should not fear death. "Truly, I say to you, today you will be with me in Paradise" (Luke 23:43). It is not just that the thief would be in paradise (heaven) after he died. Rather, it is that the thief would be in heaven *with Christ* in paradise. And it was to happen that very day. In the Greek, the word "today" is in the emphatic position, thereby indicating that there would be no delay before the repentant thief would enter heaven following death. As soon as his head dropped in death, his spirit entered the glories of paradise with the Lord Jesus! The same will be true of each of us.

Certainly Christ's faithful servant Stephen knew he would enjoy intimate fellowship with Christ upon his death. When he was being stoned to death for his faithful testimony of Jesus Christ, he looked up to heaven and said, "Lord Jesus, receive my spirit" (Acts 7:59). Once his spirit was in heaven, his direct fellowship with Christ would be perpetual and unhindered.

The apostle Paul looked forward to the same thing. In fact, Paul said, "My desire is to depart and be with Christ, for that is far better" (Philippians 1:23). This verse is incredibly rich in the original Greek. The

Greek word for "depart" was used in biblical times in reference to a ship being loosed from its moorings to sail away from the dock. The mooring that kept Paul from departing to heaven was his commitment to work among believers on earth until his assignment was complete. His ultimate desire, however, was to sail directly into God's presence. And that would happen at the moment of death.

The Greek word for "depart" was also used in biblical times for freeing someone from chains. Here on earth, you and I are chained or anchored to the hardships and heartaches of this life. In death, however, these chains are broken. We are set free for entry into heaven. At the moment of death, the spirit departs the physical body and goes directly into the presence of the Lord.

Scripture also indicates that the fellowship we have with Christ following the moment of death is nearly instant. I say this because the phrases "to depart" and "to be with Christ" are, in the original language, two sides of one coin, indicating that the very moment after Paul departs the body at death, he will be with Christ in heaven. It's a quick two-count event:

1. death on earth

2. instant fellowship with Christ in heaven

Paul communicated this same basic truth in 2 Corinthians 5:6-8: "We are always of good courage. We know that while we are at home in the body we are away from the Lord...Yes, we are of good courage, and we would rather be away from the body and at home with the Lord." This verse, too, is incredibly rich in the Greek. Without getting too technical, we might paraphrase the present tenses in the first part of this passage to say, "While we are continuing to be at home in the body while living on earth, we are continuing to be absent from the Lord." In other words, as long as we're on earth in our mortal bodies, we continue to be absent from the direct presence of the Lord in heaven.

In the latter part of the passage, however, we find two aorist infinitives instead of present tenses. We might paraphrase it this way: "We are of good courage, and prefer rather to be once-for-all absent from our flimsy, aging, and dying mortal bodies and to be once-for-all at home with the Lord in heaven." Death involves an immediate transition from being "at home in the aging mortal body" to being "away from the aging mortal body."

I want to share one more insight from the Greek with you. It has to do with the great intimacy we will have with Christ in heaven following the moment of death. In 2 Corinthians 5:8 Paul indicates that following the moment of death we are "at home with the Lord." The Greek word for "with" in this verse suggests very close (face-to-face) fellowship. It is a word typically used of intimate relationships.

So the moment you die and go to heaven, the Lord will not merely wave at you from a distance or perhaps say, "Hi, welcome to heaven," and then walk off. Rather, you will enjoy the direct, unhindered, continued, intimate presence of the Lord.

No wonder Christians need not fear death (see 1 Corinthians 15:54-55). This reminds me of a Greek I read about named Aristeides, who lived around AD 125. In a letter to a friend in which he spoke of how Christians respond to death, he wrote, "If any righteous man among the Christians passes from this world, they rejoice and offer thanks to God, and they accompany his body with songs and thanksgiving as if he were setting out from one place to another nearby." [1]

When a Christian dies today, we can truly rejoice that he or she is now in intimate fellowship with Jesus Christ. Death need not be feared!

Anticipating the Resurrection

It's awesome enough to contemplate how each of us, at the moment of death, will enter directly into the presence of God in heaven. Our spirits or souls will enjoy perpetual face-to-face intimacy with Him. But it gets even better. Indeed, as we've seen, we'll eventually also receive body upgrades, or resurrection bodies.

Our present mortal bodies could never survive in heaven's unveiled presence of God. This is why the apostle Paul said, "Flesh and blood cannot inherit the kingdom of God, nor does the perishable inherit the imperishable" (1 Corinthians 15:50). Mortal flesh is perishable and is simply not suitable to existence in heaven. The good news is that our resurrection bodies will be immortal and imperishable.

> We shall all be changed…This perishable body must put on the imperishable, and this mortal body must put on immortality. When the perishable puts on the imperishable, and the mortal puts on immortality, then shall come to pass the saying that is written: "Death is swallowed up in victory." "O death, where is your victory? O death, where is your sting?" (1 Corinthians 15:51-55).

This wondrous transition will take place on the day of the rapture (1 Thessalonians 4:13-17).

The Beatific Vision

I want to mention one final matter before closing this chapter. It has to do with what some theologians call the *beatific vision*. This term comes from a Latin phrase that means, "a happy-making sight." The idea is that beholding God in heaven brings perpetual happiness and joy to the redeemed human. Our beholding of God will not be a boring experience in which we just stare at Him. Rather, it will involve a dynamic sense of fascination as we marvel at God's perfections. Because God is infinitely perfect in His attributes, one could spend eternity contemplating them.

Oh, the wonder of being in the direct presence of God!

> OUR FATHER, *how we look forward to being face to face with You in heaven. Like the psalmist of old, we yearn to be in Your presence. We thirst to fellowship directly with You. We marvel that "in your presence there is fullness of joy; at your right hand are pleasures forevermore." We continue to ask that You grant us an eternal perspective that keeps our attention on the future joys of heaven. Thank You for the salvation You have provided for us, which will one day bring us to heaven in Your direct and unhindered presence!*

13

A Reunion of
Christian Loved Ones

You undoubtedly have Christian loved ones who have passed on in death. Over the past decade, both my mother and father have gone to be with the Lord, as have my older brother and his teenage son.

My wife, Kerri, is a schoolteacher at a Christian elementary school. One of the most heartbreaking aspects of being a teacher is that occasionally one of the elementary-age children gets a terminal illness, endures a prolonged struggle, and dies. Nothing is harder for a parent than to have to bury a young child. Nothing is more painful for a school community.

And of course, some children die while in the womb. Scripture is clear that life begins at conception (see Job 31:15; Psalm 139:13-16; Isaiah 49:1; Jeremiah 1:5). When a miscarriage or abortion occurs, the spirit of that child within the womb departs the body (at whatever developmental stage it is in) and goes directly to heaven. Kerri and I look forward to meeting two of our children who died in the womb due to miscarriages.

The crowning glory of our heavenly experience will be living in the presence of God, but we will also be rejoicing in our reunion with all our Christian loved ones and friends. We can look forward to an awesome reunion.

Insights from the Old Testament

The reuniting with other believers in the afterlife is not just a New

Testament hope. It is an Old Testament hope as well. Previously in the book, I noted that when Ishmael was 137 years old, "he breathed his last and died, and was gathered to his people" (Genesis 25:17). When the text says he was gathered to his people, the meaning is that he joined other loved ones in the afterlife who were believers.

The same thing happened with Jacob. Genesis 49:33 tells us that "when Jacob finished commanding his sons, he drew up his feet into the bed and breathed his last and was gathered to his people."

There are many similar verses in the Old Testament.

- "Isaac breathed his last, and he died and was gathered to his people" (Genesis 35:29).

- "The LORD said to Moses and Aaron at Mount Hor, on the border of the land of Edom, 'Let Aaron be gathered to his people, for he shall not enter the land that I have given to the people of Israel, because you rebelled against my command at the waters of Meribah. Take Aaron and Eleazar his son and bring them up to Mount Hor. And strip Aaron of his garments and put them on Eleazar his son. And Aaron shall be gathered to his people and shall die there" (Numbers 20:23-26).

- "The LORD said to Moses, 'Go up into this mountain of Abarim and see the land that I have given to the people of Israel. When you have seen it, you also shall be gathered to your people, as your brother Aaron was" (Numbers 27:12-13).

- "And all that generation also were gathered to their fathers" (Judges 2:10).

At death, the spirits of believers depart their bodies and are reunited with other believing family members and friends in heaven. They are "gathered to" other believers in the afterlife. As we will see, this becomes all the more clear in New Testament revelation.

Insights from the New Testament

The New Testament is brimming with insights on our future reunion in heaven with Christian loved ones and friends. In fact, we may rest assured that when Christian loved ones die, our communion with them is broken for only a short time. Our fellowship will be eternally resumed soon enough. We will again see their faces, hear their voices, and hug their (resurrected) bodies. We part with them in grief, but will be reunited in never-ending joy.

Consider the Thessalonian Christians, who were concerned about their Christian loved ones and friends who had died. They expressed their concern to the apostle Paul. So in 1 Thessalonians 4:13-17, Paul speaks about the "dead in Christ." He assures the Thessalonian Christians that there will indeed be a reunion in heaven. He says that both the dead in Christ and those Christians who are alive at the time of the rapture "will always be with the Lord" in heaven. Therefore, Paul said, they ought to comfort each other in this realization.

Certainly the apostle Paul himself expected to be reunited with his beloved Thessalonian friends in heaven. In 1 Thessalonians 2:19 he asks, "What is our hope or joy or crown of boasting before our Lord Jesus at his coming? Is it not you?" Paul rejoiced at the thought that he would be with his Thessalonian friends face to face in heaven.

We Will Recognize Each Other in the Afterlife

I believe there are clear evidences in Scripture that you and I will recognize each other in the afterlife. We just saw that Paul taught the Thessalonian Christians that they would be reunited with their Christian loved ones and that they ought to comfort one another with this reality. One must wonder what good a reunion would be if nobody recognized anybody else. I can't imagine Paul intending to say, "Rejoice, for we will be reunited with all our Christian loved ones in heaven—parents, spouses, and children—even though none of us will recognize each other." Paul's emphasis on comfort and joy is rooted in the reality that we'll be together again and recognize each other.

Second Samuel 12:23 also comes to mind. When David's son died, he expressed confidence that he would be reunited with him in heaven. "Now he is dead. Why should I fast? Can I bring him back again? I shall go to him, but he will not return to me." The fact that David would "go to him" in the afterlife clearly implies they will recognize each other and rejoice in their reunion in heaven.

Yet another passage that has relevance on this issue is Luke 16:19-31. Here Jesus speaks about the rich man and Lazarus, who died and were in the afterlife. Abraham was also there. In this passage, the rich man, Lazarus, and Abraham all recognized each other and even knew something of their histories on earth.

Yet another evidence is found in Luke 20:38, where Jesus calls God the God "of the living." In context, Jesus is talking about the God of Abraham, Isaac, and Jacob. Jesus says these patriarchs are alive and well in the afterlife. In effect, Jesus is saying, "Abraham, Isaac, and Jacob, though they died many years ago, are actually living today. For God, who calls Himself the God of Abraham, Isaac, and Jacob, is not the God of the dead but of the living."

In Matthew 8:11, Jesus says that many will eat with the Old Testament patriarchs in heaven. "Many will come from east and west and recline at table with Abraham, Isaac, and Jacob in the kingdom of heaven." This implies that Abraham, Isaac, and Jacob will still be recognized *as* Abraham, Isaac, and Jacob in heaven. Theologian Paul Enns notes that this verse pictures "Abraham reclining in the kingdom with Isaac and Jacob—his son and grandson. Family reunion! For believers, death brings a joyful reunion with believing family members. What a prospect!" [1]

Jesus's followers recognized Him after His resurrection from the dead (see John 20:26-29). Likewise, Peter, James, and John recognized the long-dead Moses and Elijah when they appeared from heaven with Jesus on the Mount of Transfiguration (see Matthew 17:1-8). These provide supportive evidence that believers recognize each other in the afterlife.

Also relevant to this discussion is 1 Corinthians 13:12, where the apostle Paul states, "Now we see in a mirror dimly, but then face to face. Now I know in part; then I shall know fully, even as I have been fully known." In ancient times, mirrors were made of polished metal and were far inferior to the mirrors we have today. The images appeared dark and indistinct. In like manner, our present knowledge is but a faint reflection of the fullness of knowledge we will have in the afterlife. This being so, we shall surely recognize our Christian loved ones and friends in the eternal state. It seems obvious that to "know fully" includes knowing names.

No Family Conflicts at This Reunion

Whenever we have family reunions during vacation times, the reunions often go just great. But let's be honest. If you're from a large family, as I am, at least a few relatives are bound to be a bit grumpy and put a bit of a strain on the reunion from time to time. I'm happy to report that such will never be the case in heaven. Our eternal reunion with Christian loved ones and friends will be ceaselessly glorious.

Keep in mind that we will no longer have sin natures. There will be no fights among loved ones. There won't be any resentment or envy or jealousy. There won't be any one-upmanship or rivalries. There won't be any cross words or misunderstandings or selfishness. Our relationships in heaven will truly be wonderful and utterly satisfying.

From a personal perspective, I so look forward to reuniting with my mother, father, brother, and all the other Christian loved ones who have preceded me in death. As much as I want to see them, however, I would never desire that they were back here on earth. After all, they are in a glorious state with no mourning, no tears, no pain, and no death, and they are enjoying direct and serene fellowship with Christ. I wouldn't even think of wanting them back here because I know they would again experience the painful turmoil that is part and parcel of life on earth. Love compels me to seek their highest good, which is found only in heaven. I will join them soon enough!

Looking for the Blessed Hope

Previously in the book I noted that in Scripture, the term "blessed hope" is a general reference to the rapture of the church. This event is blessed in the sense that it brings a sense of blessedness to the hearts of believers. The term carries the idea of joyous anticipation. Believers can hardly wait for it to happen! On that day, we will not only meet the Lord in the air but also be reunited with all our Christian loved ones and friends.

We read of this glorious event in Titus 2:13, where Christians are urged to look for "our blessed hope, the appearing of the glory of our great God and Savior Jesus Christ." The dead in Christ will be resurrected, and believers still alive on earth will be instantly translated into their resurrection bodies (see Romans 8:22-23; 1 Corinthians 15:51-58; Philippians 3:20-21; 1 Thessalonians 4:13-18; 1 John 3:2-3). These body upgrades will never again be subject to sickness, pain, and death.

As we continue to live as pilgrims just passing through this fallen world, we are empowered by this magnificent hope. Regardless of the difficulties life may throw at us, our eternal perspective keeps us going (Colossians 3:1-2).

OUR FATHER, *we are thankful beyond words that You have made the provision for us to one day be reunited with all our Christian loved ones and that we will recognize each other! We thank You that death inflicts only a temporary separation between us. We are full of gratitude in the recognition that once we are reunited in heaven, we will never again be separated, for our fellowship with each other and with You will last forever and ever. You are an awesome God!*

14

Meaningful Activities in Heaven

One of the most common questions I am asked is, what will we be doing for all eternity in heaven? Some seem to be concerned that it will be like an eternal church service, with lots of prayer, hymns, and sermons. I'm happy to say no, I don't think so!

Scripture doesn't tell us as much as we'd probably like to know about this issue, but we can derive some clear indications about our heavenly activities from the pages of Scripture. One thing is certain. We will all be involved in purposeful activities throughout eternity. But these activities will never be tiresome or tedious. In our resurrection bodies, we'll be able to work and not grow weary.

Service to God

Scripture reveals that in addition to enjoying face-to-face fellowship with God throughout eternity, we will be engaged in meaningful service to Him (Revelation 1:5-6). This service will not be toilsome or draining, but invigorating and fulfilling. We will find immeasurable satisfaction in our service to God. There will be no drudgery in heaven.

In our service to God, we won't have to rush to meet any deadlines. We won't be concerned about any time clocks. There won't be any office politics. We'll never be afraid of being fired. We will engage in our service to God without any kind of frustration and without the slightest sense of exhaustion.

This is quite a contrast to our present lives, in which we have to be exhorted by Scripture not to grow weary in doing good things (Galatians 6:9). In heaven, we will be perpetually motivated to engage in doing good things. Such exhortations will be unnecessary. We will find our service to God a truly joyful experience because we will love without measure the One we are serving. Our love for God will be our prime motivation to serve Him.

How We Live Today Matters

In Luke 19:11-26, Jesus told a parable to communicate that our service assignment in the afterlife will relate to how faithfully we serve God during our mortal life on earth. In the parable, the master says to his servant, "Because you have been faithful in a very little, you shall have authority over ten cities" (verse 17). The idea seems to be that the more faithful we are in serving God in the present life, the more we will be entrusted with in the next life in our service to God.

This has profound implications for the way we live our lives today. As Warren Wiersbe puts it, "Faithfulness now is preparation for blessed service then."[1] Bible expositor Thomas Constable agrees, noting that when Christ comes again, He will reward His followers "in proportion to what they have produced for Him...In view of what lies ahead for us we need to be steadfast, immovable, always abounding in the work of the Lord, knowing that our labor is not in vain in the Lord (1 Cor. 15:58)."[2]

Our Service Will Always Be in God's Presence

Revelation 7:15 affirms that redeemed Christians "are before the throne of God, and serve him day and night in his temple; and he who sits on the throne will shelter them with his presence." The word "temple" in this verse appears to be a metaphor pointing to the presence of God. After all, in Revelation 21:22 the apostle John affirms, "I saw no temple in the city, for its temple is the Lord God the Almighty and the Lamb." Taking these two verses together, it may well be that the reference in Revelation 7:15 to serving God day and night in His temple metaphorically means that we perpetually serve God in His presence.

Think about this. In Psalm 16:11 the psalmist affirms to God, "In your presence there is fullness of joy; at your right hand are pleasures forevermore." As we perpetually serve God in His presence, we will be full of joy and experience eternal pleasures that come from being in God's presence. How awesome it will be!

Reigning with Christ

Scripture reveals that one aspect of our service will involve reigning with Christ. Revelation 5:10 reveals that believers—God's faithful bondservants—"shall reign on the earth." This refers to faithful believers participating in the heavenly government in Christ's future millennial kingdom on earth. But our reign extends beyond the millennial kingdom into the eternal state. Indeed, Revelation 22:5 affirms that believers "will reign forever and ever." As we saw in Luke 19, a believer's position in the heavenly government will apparently be commensurate with his or her faithful service to God in the present.

Reigning with Christ appears to include judging the angels in some capacity. In 1 Corinthians 6:2-3 the apostle Paul asks, "Do you not know that the saints will judge the world?...Do you not know that we are to judge angels?" This is interesting because Psalm 8 teaches that human beings were created lower than the angels. In the afterlife, things will be reversed. Apparently the angels will be lower than redeemed humans and will be subject to their rule.

Service Not Limited to the New Earth?

God created the Garden of Eden as a perfect environment for Adam and Eve. It is hard to conceive of how perfect and ideal the Garden must have been. It must have been wondrous, for even the Lord God Himself would walk in the garden in the cool of the day (Genesis 3:8). In my mind's eye, I can imagine that the work God assigned to Adam (Genesis 2:15) must have been immeasurably enjoyable and rewarding. Adam became the steward of God's creation.

Likewise, Scripture reveals that the work God assigns to us in the new heavens and the new earth will bring immeasurable enjoyment and reward. Redeemed humans will be stewards of the new heavens and the new earth. Our service to God could possibly extend beyond the new earth to include work in the new heavens—stellar space, with its countless stars, planets, and galaxies. A number of theologians have suggested this possibility.[3] Our permanent residence will be the New Jerusalem, the eternal city of God (Revelation 3:12; 21:2), but our service to God could take us anywhere in His creation.

Fellowship with Believers We've Never Met

Here is something fascinating to think about. When we're in heaven, we'll have the opportunity to fellowship not only with Christian family members and friends but also with Christians we've never met before. This includes all the believers throughout church history, including Augustine, John Calvin, and Martin Luther. This also includes believers mentioned in the Bible, such as Adam, Noah, Abraham, Moses, Joshua, David, Solomon, Elijah, Elisha, Isaiah, the apostle John, the apostle Peter, the apostle Paul, and all the others.

Try to imagine it. We can ask Noah what building the ark was like. We can ask Moses to recount parting the Red Sea. We can ask David to describe his battle with Goliath. We can ask Peter what walking on water felt like. We can ask Martin Luther about his thoughts as he nailed the 95 theses to the door at Wittenberg. We can ask C.S. Lewis how he came up with the idea for The Chronicles of Narnia. This will be a truly fascinating aspect of life in heaven.

Praising and Worshipping God and Christ

Certainly one of the highlights of our activities in heaven will be the praise and worship of God and Jesus Christ. The Hebrew word for worship, *shaha*, means "to bow down" or "to prostrate oneself" (see Genesis 22:5; 42:6). The New Testament word for worship, *proskuneo*, also means "to prostrate oneself" (see Matthew 2:2,8,11). In Old English, "worship" was rendered "worthship," pointing to the worthiness of the God we worship. Such worship is the proper response of a creature to the divine Creator (Psalm 95:6).

We already know that the angels ceaselessly worship the Lord (see Revelation 4:8). The apostle John speaks of a hundred million angels singing praises in unison to the God they adore (Revelation 5:11-12).

But one day, countless redeemed humans will join the company of angels in singing praise and rendering worship to God (Revelation 7:9-10; see also 4:8; 5:8-13; 14:2-3; 15:1-4). Revelation 19:1-6 portrays a great multitude of believers worshipfully shouting out "Hallelujah" before God's throne.

Let me be quick to say that the worship of God in heaven will not be a tedious or contrived experience, as it sometimes is in church services. I'm sure we've all experienced worship on Sunday mornings that has seemed superficial and even (dare I say) boring. Worship in heaven, however, will be utterly genuine, spontaneous, and exhilarating. It will be wondrous. Our lips will be full of adoration to His name. Being in our awesome God's direct presence will make all the difference.

Learning More About Our Incomparable God

Yet another activity in heaven will involve learning ever more about our awesome God. Redeemed human beings will not be omniscient (or all-knowing) in the afterlife like God is. Our knowledge and capacity to understand will apparently be greatly increased (see 1 Corinthians 13:12), but we will not be omniscient. This means that you and I will still be able to grow in knowledge in the afterlife. One area where we are sure to grow in knowledge relates to our awesome God and His countless perfections. Even now, the angels continue to learn about God and His ways (see 1 Peter 1:12). The same will be true of redeemed human beings once we are in heaven.

Scripture affirms that God is "the One who is high and lifted up, who inhabits eternity, whose name is Holy" (Isaiah 57:15). Scripture asks, "Who has known the mind of the Lord, or who has been his counselor?" (Romans 11:34). Paul speaks of Jesus Christ, "in whom are hidden all the treasures of wisdom and knowledge" (Colossians 2:3). We will be ceaselessly enriched as we continue learning more and more about our wondrous God throughout eternity.

This means you and I will never be bored in heaven. God has so many matchless perfections that we will always be learning new and wonderful things about Him. We will never come to the end of exploring Him and His marvelous riches. This will be a constant cause of amazement to us.

Enjoying Rest

There will certainly be plenty of rest in heaven as well (Revelation 14:13). I cannot help but think that having a restful existence is part and parcel of being in the presence of Jesus Christ for all eternity. After all, Jesus once told His followers, "Come to me, all who labor and are heavy laden, and I will give you rest" (Matthew 11:28). Our present lives are under the tyranny of the urgent. But in heaven, such urgency will be a thing of the distant past, and we will forever dwell in the presence of the eternal rest-giver, Jesus Christ.

A Closing Reflection

You've no doubt come across a common caricature of the afterlife that pictures a person sitting on the clouds of heaven while playing a harp. I don't know about you, but if I had to play a harp while sitting on a cloud for all eternity, that would get old real quick!

Of course, such an idea has no basis in Scripture. Rather, as we've seen above, our existence in heaven will be filled with a wide variety of meaningful and joyful activities.

I am also sure there will be many activities in heaven that I've not even touched on in this chapter. But I believe all our experiences will be full of wonder and awe. As one of my favorite verses puts it, we will experience "what no eye has seen, nor ear heard, nor the heart of man imagined" (1 Corinthians 2:9).

Our Father, *our minds cannot even begin to comprehend the wonder of what is to come for each of us as Your children. We praise You and worship You not only for what You've prepared for us in the future but also because of who You are—the wonderful Creator, whose name is Yahweh, the Most High, the Strong One, God Almighty. You are everlasting and high and lifted up. The reality that we will one day be face to face with You staggers our minds, but we are so thankful for this wondrous future.*
We exalt You, O Lord.

15

No Need to Fear Death

Most people have a natural fear of death. Even for those of us who are Christians, death brings a sense of dread. This is reflected in the apostle Paul's affirmation that death is the last enemy to be conquered (1 Corinthians 15:26; see also Isaiah 25:8). Death, as an enemy, is no respecter of persons. Every human becomes a target of the grim reaper—the righteous and the wicked, the rich and the poor, men and women, and people of all skin colors. People of every nation on earth are targeted.

Our concern over death escalates as we grow older. As we look in the mirror, we see relentless signs of aging—signs that our bodies are slowly but surely wearing out. We are all acutely aware that we have no guarantee of living a long life. Some people drop from a heart attack in their twenties. Others in their eighties or nineties. Death could come at any time.

As we examine the pages of Scripture, we find many people of God who expressed fear of the impending reality of death. Job, for example, referred to death as "the king of terrors" (Job 18:14). The psalmist lamented, "My heart is in anguish within me; the terrors of death have fallen upon me" (Psalm 55:4). The psalmist also reflected, "The snares of death encompassed me; the pangs of Sheol laid hold on me; I suffered distress and anguish" (Psalm 116:3). Jesus's own disciples cried out to Jesus in the boat during a severe storm, "Save us, Lord; we are perishing" (Matthew 8:25).

I often think about Hezekiah, who was a godly king of Judah.

When Isaiah informed him that his death was impending, he was grief-stricken and wept bitterly (2 Kings 20:1-11; see also Isaiah 38:9-13). He poured out his heart to God, and in this particular case, God intervened and extended his life another 15 years. This, of course, is not the norm.

Death has a long history of enslaving people in fear. One of the reasons Christ came into the world was to "deliver all those who through fear of death were subject to lifelong slavery" (Hebrews 2:15). This verse reveals that God does not want those who trust in Christ for salvation to fear death.

Of course, as I noted previously in the book, one generation of Christians will escape death altogether. I'm referring to Christians who are alive on earth when the rapture occurs. All other Christians will pass through death's door. It may come suddenly and unexpectedly because of a car wreck, an accident, or a deadly stroke. In other cases, it may approach slowly, and we see it coming, perhaps due to a cancer or some other fatal illness.

If we are honest, most of us would admit that we've thought about what death might be like. Will it be quick? Will the process of dying take a long time? Will pain be involved? Will our loved ones be able to care for us in our final days? Will we need hospice care? Truthfully, many people are more afraid of the process of dying than they are the actual death itself. I once heard Joni Eareckson Tada speak of this fear in her own life.

Death Has Been Conquered

The good news is that we need not fear death, for death is a conquered enemy. One of my favorite psalms is Psalm 23, where David the shepherd exulted, "Even though I walk through the valley of the shadow of death, I will fear no evil, for you are with me; your rod and your staff, they comfort me." One of the important lessons we glean from this verse is that our divine Shepherd is with us not only at the actual moment of death but also during the process of walking through the valley of the shadow of death. We never go it alone. Our Lord is with us during life, and He will be with us during the process of dying. Once the moment actually comes, we will be face to face with Him in heaven (Philippians 1:21-23). It is an event to anticipate with joy.

As one theologian once put it, death is not a *terminus*, but rather a *tunnel* that leads to a resplendently glorious heaven (see 2 Corinthians 5:1-8). Thus, death for the believer involves a wondrous transition, not a final condition. Death marks the beginning of a wondrous new life in heaven with Christ that will last forever. Death is a gateway into eternal life, and once we are there, death will never again surface among the redeemed.

Recall the apostle Paul's words in Philippians 1:23: "My desire is to depart and be with Christ, for that is far better." Paul was speaking from experience. Second Corinthians 12:2-4 informs us that during his earthly ministry Paul had been caught up to paradise. The word "paradise" literally means "garden of pleasure" or "garden of delight." Revelation 2:7 refers to heaven as the "paradise of God." Paul said he "was caught up into paradise" and "heard things that cannot be told, which man may not utter."

Apparently this paradise of God is so resplendently glorious, so ineffable, so wondrous, that Paul was forbidden to say anything about it to those still in the earthly realm. But what Paul saw instilled in him an eternal perspective that enabled him to face the trials that lay ahead of him. He not only did not fear death, he could hardly wait for it to happen so he could get back to the heavenly paradise.

As he recalled and pondered how wondrous and glorious paradise was, he could easily say that he desired to depart this life so he could be with Christ in heaven. No wonder he faced his martyrdom with a cheerful serenity (2 Timothy 4:6-8). He had no worries. He knew where he was going. He knew that in a flash, at the moment of his death, he'd be right back in heaven, where he had previously visited.

Moreover, let us not forget the New Testament teaching regarding our body upgrades. In view of our coming resurrection, we ought to view death as a conquered enemy. "When the perishable puts on the imperishable, and the mortal puts on immortality, then shall come to pass the saying that is written: 'Death is swallowed up in victory.' 'O death, where is your victory? O death, where is your sting?'" (1 Corinthians 15:54-55).

Because of what Christ accomplished at the cross and His subsequent resurrection from the dead, we need never be terrorized by death's ever-present threat again. Because Christ is risen, we too shall rise! Our destiny is heaven! For the Christian, physical death is a quick step into life, life, and more life.

Let Not Your Heart Be Troubled

Jesus informed His followers that they need not fear His death or their own, for one day they'd be together again in the afterlife in a place He Himself is preparing.

> Let not your hearts be troubled. Believe in God; believe also in me. In my Father's house are many rooms. If it were not so, would I have told you that I go to prepare a place for you? And if I go and prepare a place for you, I will come again and will take you to myself, that where I am you may be also (John 14:1-3).

These verses refer to the rapture. The rapture is that glorious event in which the dead in Christ will be resurrected, the living Christians will be instantly translated into their resurrection bodies, and both groups will be caught up to meet Christ in the air and taken back to heaven (1 Corinthians 15:51-54; 1 Thessalonians 4:13-17). In view of this imminent event, Jesus instructed His followers, "Let not your hearts be troubled."

God will walk with us through the death experience. God will not abandon us in our darkest earthly moment. He will most certainly give us strength when we have none of our own. He will certainly give us His courage when we feel cowardly. He will certainly bring us comfort when we are hurting. Never forget that we will not be alone in death!

Never Again Will We Face Death

Once we pass through death's door, we will never have to pass through it again. Indeed, God "will wipe away every tear from their eyes, and death shall be no more, neither shall there be mourning nor crying nor pain anymore, for the former things have passed away" (Revelation 21:4). The very moment we breathe our last breath on earth, we enter an utterly deathless state. One moment we might be walking through the dark valley of the shadow of death, only to suddenly discover that we are now in the kingdom of light that is ruled by the light of the world, Jesus Christ. One moment we might be struggling in a state of weakness and perhaps terminal sickness, and the next moment find ourselves with strength and health in heaven. In view of such a wondrous future, why should we fear death?

Waiting with Anticipation

The anticipation of entering heaven is altogether sweet for those who hold Christ dear to their hearts. Dear saint of God, fear not that you will die. Your Savior has you in His hands in both life and death. All is in His sovereign care. Trust Him.

God instructs His people, "Fear not, for I am with you; be not dismayed, for I am your God; I will strengthen you, I will help you, I will uphold you with my righteous right hand" (Isaiah 41:10; see also Philippians 4:6-7). It is good to meditate on this and other verses that fuel an eternal perspective in our hearts and lives. Here are some of my favorites.

- "This light momentary affliction is preparing for us an eternal weight of glory beyond all comparison, as we look not to the things that are seen but to the things that are unseen. For the things that are seen are transient, but the things that are unseen are eternal" (2 Corinthians 4:17-18).

- "Blessed be the God and Father of our Lord Jesus Christ! According to his great mercy, he has caused us to be born again to a living hope through the resurrection of Jesus Christ from the dead, to an inheritance that is imperishable, undefiled, and unfading, kept in heaven for you" (1 Peter 1:3-4).

- "I consider that the sufferings of this present time are not worth comparing with the glory that is to be revealed to us" (Romans 8:18).

- "We know that if the tent [our present mortal body] that is our earthly home is destroyed, we have a building from

God [a resurrection body], a house not made with hands, eternal in the heavens. For in this tent we groan, longing to put on our heavenly dwelling" (2 Corinthians 5:1-2).

Rejoice, for "our citizenship is in heaven" (Philippians 3:20).

OUR FATHER, *how thankful we are that our true citizenship is in heaven. We are grateful that we need not be dismayed by death, for You will be with us every step of the way. We are thankful for the glorious inheritance that awaits us in heaven. We marvel that once we are with You in heaven, great glory will be revealed in us. We also greatly anticipate the resurrection of our bodies. In view of such promises, enable us, O Lord, to live without a fear of death. Thank You, Lord.*

16

Heaven for Infants and Young Children Who Die

I became very interested in the issue of infant salvation when my wife and I suffered two miscarriages in the 1990s. Of course, while in seminary in the early 1980s, I gathered a lot of head knowledge related to the issue. For example, I learned that Scripture portrays the baby in the womb as a genuine human being with an eternal soul (Exodus 21:22-24; Psalm 139:13-15; Jeremiah 1:5). But our miscarriages forced me to take the theology much more personally. Since then, I've met many people who have suffered through this same heartbreaking experience.

Nowadays, I've grown to consider this issue as one of profound importance because of the number of infant deaths, miscarriages, and sadly, abortions around the world. Scripture portrays the baby in the womb as a living human being—body and eternal soul—so we must consider both born and unborn infants in this chapter.

Because of the staggering number of infant deaths around the world, it is understandable that Christian parents express concern about their eternal destiny. The issue for Christian parents is this: If faith in Christ is required for salvation, and if infants lack the capacity to exercise faith, what are we to conclude about whether they are saved? I might add that we can ask the same question of people with cognitive disabilities. The ultimate question is, what about heaven for those who can't believe?

An Issue of Debate

Not surprisingly, this issue has seen much theological debate. Various solutions have been suggested.

Some believe that infants and young children are automatically saved simply because they seem to be sinless. The problem for this viewpoint is that they are *not* sinless. Scripture portrays all human beings (since the Fall) as born into the world with a sin nature and a sin problem (see Psalm 14:1; Romans 3:23; 5:12; James 3:2; 1 John 1:8-10).

Others find the solution in the love of God. It is suggested that because God is characterized by pure love, He would never send an infant to hell. It is true that God is loving (1 John 4:8), but this view fails to consider God's equally important attribute of holiness (1 Peter 1:16). We must not forget that God never bases an action on just one attribute to the exclusion of others. More to the point, God never abandons holiness in order to be loving. Infants are born into the world with a sin nature, and this is something that God in His holiness cannot simply ignore.

Still others base their solution on God's foreknowledge. In this view, God looks down the corridors of time at the hypothetical future of the dead child and assesses whether or not that child would have trusted in Christ had he continued living. Those babies who would have trusted in Christ are deemed saved, and those who would not have trusted in Christ are deemed unsaved.

I realize that all of these viewpoints come from sincere Christians who are trying to make sense of an extremely difficult issue. But I must be honest in saying that I think they all have some serious theological deficiencies. In what follows, I will provide good reasons for concluding that infants who die are immediately ushered into God's glorious presence in heaven.

All Need to Be Saved

We begin with the recognition that all of Scripture points to the universal need of salvation, for all people are universally lost in sin. This includes infants and small children.

Of course, as we hold newborn infants in our arms, they have incredibly smooth skin and silky-smooth hair. They are soft and cuddly and make endearing cooing sounds. Nevertheless, the cancer of sin lurks deep within. From a Scriptural perspective, every one of us—including every infant—is lost (Luke 19:10), perishing (John 3:16), condemned (John 3:18), and under God's wrath (John 3:36),

You and I have a sin nature from the moment of conception. In Psalm 51:5, David affirmed of himself, "Behold, I was brought forth in iniquity, and in sin did my mother conceive me." This does not mean that David's mother somehow sinned in becoming pregnant with David. Rather, it means that from the moment David was conceived, iniquity was deep within him.

This is why the New Testament categorically states that all human beings are "by nature children of wrath" (Ephesians 2:3). All are born in sin (1 Corinthians 15:22). "None is righteous, no, not one" (Romans 3:10).

We therefore must avoid thinking that infants are born into the world in a sinless state. The same sin that bars me from heaven also bars young infants from heaven. One of my professors at Dallas Theological Seminary used to say that infants are lovely but lost, delightful but depraved. Therefore, the solution to infant salvation must be found in other theological considerations.

The Age of Accountability

On the one hand, infants are born into the world in a state of sin. On the other hand, young infants are *not* portrayed in Scripture as morally culpable beings—not until they reach the age of accountability.

But what is the age of accountability? It's not the same for every child. Some children mature faster than others. Some come into an awareness of personal evil and righteousness earlier than others do.

James 4:17 gets to the heart of the matter: "Whoever knows the right thing to do and fails to do it, for him it is sin." This verse implies that when a child comes into a personal awareness of "oughts" and "shoulds," he or she has reached the age of accountability and therefore becomes morally accountable to God.

I believe that all infants who die before the age of accountability are automatically saved and are issued directly into the presence of the Lord in heaven upon the moment of death. There is good reason to conclude that at the moment infants die (and not before) the benefits of Jesus's atoning death on the cross are applied to them. At that moment, the infants become saved and are immediately issued into the presence of God in heaven. This view is in keeping with not only the love of God but also His holiness. I provide the theological justification for this view below.

God's Purpose in Salvation

In reading the New Testament, especially the writings of the apostle Paul, we find a predominant emphasis on the grace of God in salvation. Ephesians 1:7-8 reveals that one of the primary purposes of God in saving human beings is to display His wondrous grace "in all wisdom and insight." This being the case, one naturally wonders how such wondrous grace could ever be seen as compatible with sending infants to hell. And how could such an act ever be considered compatible with God's "wisdom and insight"?

It would be a cruel mockery for God to call upon infants to do what they could not do—and to hold them responsible for that. At such a young age, children simply do not have the capacity to exercise saving faith in Christ.

Infants Are Never Portrayed in Hell

It is an educational experience to use a concordance to look up every single reference to hell in the Bible. This exercise yields the conclusion that not a single verse indicates that infants and young children are there. Only adults capable of making decisions are portrayed as being there.

In keeping with this, infants and young children are not mentioned as participating in the judgment of the wicked dead—the great white throne judgment (Revelation 20:11-15). The complete silence of Scripture regarding infants being judged or being in hell must be taken to mean that they are simply not there.

Jesus Loves Little Children

Because of Jesus's identity as God, we get a feel for God's heart toward children in the words of Jesus. Consider Matthew 18:1-14.

> The disciples came to Jesus, saying, "Who is the greatest in the kingdom of heaven?" And calling to him a child, he put him in the midst of them and said, "Truly, I say to you, unless you turn and become like children, you will never enter the kingdom of heaven. Whoever humbles himself like this child is the greatest in the kingdom of heaven.
>
> Whoever receives one such child in my name receives me, but whoever causes one of these little ones who believe in me to sin, it would be better for him to have a great mill-stone fastened around his neck and to be drowned in the depth of the sea...
>
> See that you do not despise one of these little ones...It is not the will of my Father who is in heaven that one of these little ones should perish."

The little children never opposed Jesus in the slightest. All of them allowed Jesus to do with them as He pleased. There was no rejection on their part. And oh, how Jesus loved them! How very much Jesus loved the little children! We are even told that people must become like the little children to enter God's kingdom. All things considered, I do not see how someone could read Matthew 18:1-14 and conclude that it is within the realm of possibility that Jesus could damn such little ones to hell!

The Attributes of God

The attributes of God provide supportive evidence for the salvation of infants.

Wisdom. God in His infinite wisdom sovereignly decreed a plan designed to bring the most glory to Himself (Job 12:13; Psalm 104:24; Proverbs 3:19; Romans 11:33; 16:27; James 3:17). God would certainly not be glorified by condemning little infants and mentally disabled people who died and who were incapable of placing saving faith in Christ.

Love. God is characterized by love. We read in 1 John 4:16, "We have come to know and to believe the love that God has for us. God is love." God not only loves, He *is* love. And it is in keeping with the love of God to incorporate in the plan of salvation a means of saving those who, though sinful, are utterly incapable of believing in Him.

Mercy and grace. God is full of mercy (Psalms 116:5; 136:1; Lamentations 3:22-24; Romans 9:16; 2 Corinthians 1:3; Ephesians 2:4-5) and grace (Exodus 34:6; Nehemiah 9:17; Psalm 103:8; Ephesians 2:8-9; Titus 2:11; 1 Peter 5:10). "Mercy" refers to the withholding of deserved punishment. "Grace" refers to God's undeserved favor. God not only shows undeserved favor to people but also withholds deserved punishment. How could God be gracious and merciful if He failed to incorporate in the plan of salvation a means of saving those who are sinful but utterly incapable of believing in Him?

Goodness. Nahum 1:7 affirms that "the Lord is good." Psalm 31:19 exclaims, "How abundant is your goodness." Surely God in His goodness would not require of an infant something the infant could not possibly do—that is, exercise faith for salvation. God in His goodness would surely incorporate in the plan of salvation a means of saving sinful individuals who are utterly incapable of believing in Him.

Justice. All God's actions are fair and just (Genesis 18:25; Psalm 11:7; Romans 3:26; Hebrews 6:10). Zephaniah 3:5 affirms that God "does no injustice; every morning he shows forth his justice." Psalm 103:6 exclaims, "The Lord works righteousness and justice for all who are oppressed." Surely the Lord in His justice and righteousness would not demand of infants something that they were utterly incapable of— that is, exercising saving faith. It would be righteous and just for God to make other provisions for them.

Now, here is something to think about. From a scriptural perspective, God's wrath comes upon people only because they refuse God's way of escape. This means that human beings ultimately choose God's wrath for themselves. It is poured out only on those who choose to be His enemies. Those who are incapable of believing in Him are not His enemies! Infants lack the ability to choose, so they cannot possibly be the objects of God's wrath.

It makes infinitely more sense to say that God—who is characterized by wisdom, love, mercy, grace, and goodness—incorporated in His plan of salvation a means of saving those who are sinful but are utterly incapable of believing in Him. The salvation of infants is therefore in complete keeping with the attributes of God.

King David and His Son

King David believed he would be reconciled with his dead infant son in heaven. He affirmed: "While the child was still alive, I fasted and wept, for I said, 'Who knows whether the LORD will be gracious to me, that the child may live?' But now he is dead. Why should I fast? Can I bring him back again? I shall go to him, but he will not return to me." David here affirmed that when he died, he would go to be with his son in heaven.

The Basis of the Judgment of the Lost

The basis of the judgment of the lost provides yet another supportive evidence that infants and young children who die go to heaven. Consider the description of this judgment in Revelation 20:11-13.

> Then I saw a great white throne and him who was seated on it. From his presence earth and sky fled away, and no place was found for them. And I saw the dead, great and small, standing before the throne, and books were opened. Then another book was opened, which is the book of life. And the dead were judged by what was written in the books, according to what they had done. And the sea gave up the dead who were in it, Death and Hades gave up the dead who were in them, and they were judged, each one of them, according to what they had done.

Notice that these people are judged "according to what they had done" (compare with Psalm 62:12; Proverbs 24:12; Matthew 16:27; Romans 2:6; 2 Corinthians 5:10; Revelation 2:23). Infants and young children have no moral awareness and are not responsible for the deeds they commit, so this judgment must be inapplicable to them.

Assessing the Evidence

My conclusion is simple and straightforward. Heaven receives those who can't believe. If a child should die before reaching the age of accountability, the benefits of Christ's death are applied to that child at the moment of death, and the child is issued immediately into the presence of God in heaven. This includes preborn babies—that is, babies who die in the womb due to a miscarriage or an abortion.

> OUR FATHER, *we rejoice in the truth that in Jesus, "we have redemption through his blood, the forgiveness of our trespasses, according to the riches of his grace, which he lavished upon us, in all wisdom and insight." We are so very thankful for the infinite wisdom and insight that was exercised in bringing about our salvation, including that of infants. We are forever grateful that our salvation is based entirely upon Your wonderful grace. We marvel that You are such a merciful God. We praise You, O Lord.*

Assessing Personal Visits to Heaven

A visit to heaven has become one of the hottest-selling topics in nonfiction today. Don Piper's *90 Minutes in Heaven*, Todd Burpo and Lynn Vincent's *Heaven Is for Real: A Little Boy's Astounding Story of His Trip to Heaven and Back*, and Mary Neal's *To Heaven and Back: A Doctor's Extraordinary Account of Her Death, Heaven, Angels, and Life Again* all come to mind. Such books regularly find themselves on the *New York Times* bestseller list.

What are we to make of such accounts? On the one hand, the people writing such books claim to be Christians, and we therefore want to give them the benefit of the doubt regarding the truthfulness of their books. On the other hand, the Bible is our sole basis of authority—not only for our view of heaven, but for all doctrines. This means that regardless of who has written firsthand reports of what heaven is actually like, we must test the claims against the Bible.

These Are Not Actual Deaths

We must be careful to note that these experiences are categorized as near-death experiences, not once-for-all, truly-and-completely-dead experiences. As one Christian apologist noted, we may learn no more about death from near-death experiences than we learn about Denver from reports by someone who has never been within the actual city limits. In both cases (Denver and death), more reliable "maps" are available. In the case of death and the afterlife, the only truly reliable map is Scripture.[1]

Things "Which Man May Not Utter"

Sometime during his ministry, the apostle Paul was caught up to heaven. While there, "he heard things that cannot be told, which man may not utter" (2 Corinthians 12:4). The question that naturally comes to mind is this: If the apostle Paul was forbidden to describe what he witnessed in heaven and was instructed that "no man" may utter these things, why is it that multiple modern writers are allowed to write about their alleged prolonged visits to heaven? This question is especially relevant considering that these modern writers are not apostles, as Paul was.

The *Believer's Bible Commentary* instructs that "Paul heard the language of Paradise and understood what was spoken, but he was not allowed to repeat any of it when he came back to the earth. The words were inexpressible in the sense that they were too sacred to be uttered and therefore not for publication."[2]

We can also observe that Lazarus did not speak about the afterlife after Jesus resurrected him from the dead (John 11). In fact, biblical accounts of those raised from the dead are never accompanied by heavenly travel testimonials (1 Kings 17:17-24; 2 Kings 4:18-37; Matthew 9:19-26; Luke 7:11-15; Acts 9:36-43; 20:9-12).

Earthly minds may simply be unable to fully comprehend heavenly realities. In John 3:12 Jesus Himself stated, "If I have told you earthly things and you do not believe, how can you believe if I tell you heavenly things?" Paul commented that "no eye has seen, nor ear heard, nor the heart of man imagined, what God has prepared for those who love him" (1 Corinthians 2:9). Such verses do not prove that modern writers have not had some kind of heavenly experience, but they do call for caution and discernment when evaluating them.

No Adding to Scripture

Christians ought to be especially careful in evaluating heavenly experiences in view of the stern warnings in the Bible about adding to the Word of God. A great deal about what the Bible reveals about heaven is found in the book of Revelation. And in this book, we are explicitly warned against adding to what is written.

> I warn everyone who hears the words of the prophecy of this book: if anyone adds to them, God will add to him the plagues described in this book, and if anyone takes away from the words of the book of this prophecy, God will take away his share in the tree of life and in the holy city, which are described in this book (Revelation 22:18-19).

Granted, no one writing books today is claiming that their books belong in the Bible. Still, one could argue that these new "revelations" about heaven, which supplement what we read in the Bible, may come perilously close to violating the spirit of this passage. At the very least, this scriptural warning in Revelation calls for caution and discernment in evaluating such experiences.

Contradictory "Revelations"

Please be assured that my goal is not to go on a witch hunt or to undermine these recent books. However, inasmuch as the Bible is our sole authority on matters of faith and practice, we must always be like the Bereans and test all spiritual claims against Scripture (Acts 17:11; see also 1 Thessalonians 5:21).

With this in mind, consider that Don Piper's book *90 Minutes in Heaven* describes the physical attributes of his late grandfather Joe Kulbeth—including his white hair and "big banana nose." Biblically, when believers die, their spirit departs the body and goes to heaven (2 Corinthians 5:8; Philippians 1:21-23; Revelation 6:9-10). Departed believers will not receive physical resurrection bodies until the day of the rapture (1 Thessalonians 4:13-17).

Piper also made some rather odd statements in his book. He claims there is constant music in heaven, like thousands of songs all at once that somehow blend into a perfect, glorious symphony. Moreover, in his book he said he did not see God in heaven. But in the years since, while speaking in churches, he has stated that he saw God. What are we to make of such contradictions?

In Todd Burpo and Lynn Vincent's *Heaven Is for Real*, we find that Christians who die and go to heaven have wings and a halo. God is also described as a "very big person." The book also states, "The Scripture says that as Jesus gave up His spirit (on the cross)…God the Father turned his back. I am convinced that he did that because if he had kept on watching, he couldn't have gone through with it." [3] The plan of salvation seems to have been in potential jeopardy. The Scriptures give a different perspective.

- Not a single verse says that believers have wings or halos in the afterlife. Halos began appearing in Christian art in the fourth century.

- The description of God as a "very big person" could conflict with the biblical reality that God is a spirit (John 4:24) and is invisible (Colossians 1:15; 1 Timothy 6:16).

- The idea that the Father had to turn his back on His Son's suffering, or else He might not have been able to go through with it, makes God's plan of salvation seem tenuous and liable to collapse. By contrast, Scripture portrays human salvation as an outworking of God's unbending and absolute sovereign decree (see Isaiah 46:10; Acts 2:23; 1 Corinthians 15:23-28; Ephesians 1:11; 1 Peter 1:20).

I could discuss other problematic issues related to some of these recent books, but in the interest of being gracious, I will decline. I urge you, however, to test all things against Scripture when reading experiential accounts of heaven. Scripture will keep you on the right track.

Are Near-Death Experiences in the Bible?

Through the years, a number of people have claimed that Scripture includes reports of near-death experiences. Acts 9:3-6 is often suggested.

> Now as he [Saul] went on his way, he approached Damascus, and suddenly a light from heaven shone around him.

And falling to the ground he heard a voice saying to him, "Saul, Saul, why are you persecuting me?" And he said, "Who are you, Lord?" And he said, "I am Jesus, whom you are persecuting. But rise and enter the city, and you will be told what you are to do."

Sometime later, Saul became a Christian, and his name was changed to Paul. He eventually had a discussion with King Agrippa in which he alluded to this same experience (Acts 26:12-18). A number of points argue against the idea that Paul had a near-death experience in these verses.

1. Most obviously, Paul was quite alive and nowhere near dying. By no stretch of the imagination, then, can this be called a near-death experience.

2. The light literally blinded Paul (Acts 9:8)—something completely unlike a typical near-death experience of today. In fact, in the history of near-death experiences, no one has claimed to be literally blinded. Modern books claim that heaven is luminescent but not that it is overwhelmingly so.

3. In his later discussion with King Agrippa, Paul never mentioned anything remotely resembling a near-death experience.

4. Unlike modern visit-to-heaven books in which the gospel is conspicuously absent, Jesus commissioned Paul to evangelize so that people may receive forgiveness of sins by faith in Jesus and thereby escape the fires of hell.

Only one conclusion is possible. This passage does not describe a near-death experience.

False Doctrines from a "Being of Light"

Many people who are not necessarily Christians have also had near-death experiences in which they've claimed to encounter a being of light, whom they believed to be Jesus. The fatal flaw here is that this being typically says things contrary to what the Christ of the Bible would say.

- Sin is not a problem.

- There is no hell to worry about.

- All people are welcome in heaven regardless of whether they have placed faith in Christ.

- All religions are equally valid.

Jesus is the same yesterday, today, and forever (Hebrews 13:8), so the Jesus of the Bible would never say such things. For this reason, I have no alternative but to conclude that many of the people who have had near-death experiences have actually encountered a counterfeit Christ (see 2 Corinthians 11:14-15; compare with John 8:44).

The Possible Connection with Occultism

A number of Christian researchers have noted a connection between near-death experiences and occultism. John Weldon and John Ankerberg, for example, claim that the near-death experience is largely one form of the occult out-of-body experience (OBE). They claim that both kinds of experiences can, in some cases, lead to spiritistic contact, worldview changes, and the development of psychic powers. [4]

In keeping with this, near-death researcher Kenneth Ring documents that people frequently experience "psychic events" following a near-death experience. He documents the claim of many that their "psychic sensitivities have developed strikingly" since their near-death experiences. [5] Others have reported the emergence of clairvoyance* and telepathy† following such experiences. Some have even claimed to encounter spirit guides.

Of course, in Scripture, God strongly condemns occultism and

---

* Clairvoyance involves the ability to see something beyond natural means about the past, present, or future.

† Telepathy involves the receiving or sending of thoughts to another person.

psychic phenomena. Anyone doubting this should meditate on Deuteronomy 18:10-13, Galatians 5:19-21, and Revelation 21:8.

Are Any Visit-to-Heaven Experiences Legitimate?

In view of all the above, you may be thinking that I reject virtually all claims of near-death experiences. This is not the case, however. What I've written above is designed to impress upon you the importance of caution and discernment on this experiential issue.

Now that I've done that, allow me to close by touching on possible legitimate near-death experiences. Researcher Jerry Yamamoto is probably right in his assessment that since near-death experiences "are of a subjective nature, determining their source is largely a speculative venture. With divine, demonic, and several natural factors all meriting considerations, a single, universal explanation for near-death experiences becomes quite risky." [6]

I am aware of a number of Christian researchers who suggest that while we must be extremely cautious on this issue, some people may have actually had bona fide near-death experiences with the genuine Jesus. This group would especially include Christians as well as people who became Christians as a direct result of the encounter.

Yamamoto suggests, "If the message and experience of a near-death experience does not distort or conflict with biblical teachings, then we should be careful not to speak against that which resulted in salvation and may have been a genuine work of God." [7] Yamamoto cites a case in which he thinks this is in fact what occurred. (A man named Dan became a devout Christian immediately after his near-death experience.)

Christian apologists Gary R. Habermas and J.P. Moreland, after an exhaustive study, concluded, "Just as you can't have fake money without real money, so you can't have fake near-death experiences without real ones. You can't counterfeit what doesn't exist." [8] Their point is that even though there are many counterfeit near-death experiences that portray a counterfeit Jesus who preaches a counterfeit message, so there are some genuine near-death experiences in which people may have actually encountered the true Jesus. It would appear that the great evangelist Dwight L. Moody had a genuine near-death experience.

My best advice is this: No matter what kind of experience is claimed, always test it against Scripture. Be cautious and discerning. If anything contradicts the Word of God, it must be rejected outright. Make Scripture your sole measuring stick. The Scriptures will keep you safe and on track. You can also pray that God will give you wisdom (James 1:5; see also 1 Kings 3:1-15). If in your discerning examination you come across a near-death account you feel is legitimate and plausible, and there are no biblical "red flags" or theological concerns, you can rejoice in this possible work of God.

> OUR FATHER, *we are so thankful that You have given us Your Word, which is a lamp to our feet. Your Word is like a barometer of truth against which we can test all other truth claims. Toward this end, we seek to be like the Bereans, who tested all teachings against the Word of God. We seek to follow the apostle Paul's admonition to test all things and to retain only that which is true. Keep us on the path of truth regarding all the doctrines of Scripture, including the afterlife. We are grateful to You, O Lord.*

Unbelievers at the Great White Throne Judgment

The judgment seat of Christ pertains only to believers. At this judgment, the Lord Jesus either dispenses or withholds rewards among the redeemed. It's all based on the Christian's level of faithfulness during earthly life.

Unlike this judgment, the great white throne judgment awaits unbelievers of all ages. It is a horrific judgment that leads to their being cast into the lake of fire (Revelation 20:11-15). The Judge is Jesus Christ, for the Father has committed all judgment to Him (Matthew 19:28; John 5:22-30; Acts 10:42; 17:31). Those who are judged are the unsaved dead of all ages.

This throne is "great" because the One who sits on it is our "great God and Savior," Jesus Christ (Titus 2:13-14). It is white, suggesting that the One who sits on the throne is holy, pure, and righteous (see Psalm 97:2; Daniel 7:9).

The judgment takes place after the millennial kingdom, Christ's 1000-year reign on planet earth. We know this because Revelation 20, after describing the millennium, states, "Then I saw a great white throne and him who was seated on it" (verse 11).

As to where this judgment takes place, theologian Charles Ryrie suggests that "a great white throne will be established somewhere in space, for the present earth and starry heavens will have been replaced."[1]

Unsaved Only

I must underscore that those who participate in this judgment are here precisely because they are already unsaved. Those judged are simply called "the dead" in obvious contrast to "the dead in Christ."

This means that this judgment will not separate believers from unbelievers, for all who will experience it will have already made the choice during their lifetimes to reject God. The fact that people arrive at this judgment is sorrowful beyond measure, for they have no chance of redemption. They are there because they are unsaved, and they are about to be cast into the lake of fire. I cannot even begin to imagine the sense of dread that will permeate the minds of those who will be there.

Warren Wiersbe provides these words of wisdom regarding the necessity of hell (the lake of fire).

> Hell is a witness to the righteous character of God. He must judge sin. Hell is also a witness to man's responsibility, the fact that he is not a robot or a helpless victim, but a creature able to make choices. God does not "send people to hell"; they send themselves by rejecting the Savior (Matt. 25:41; John 3:16–21). Hell is also a witness to the awfulness of sin. If we once saw sin as God sees it, we would understand why a place such as hell exists.[2]

Theologian J.I. Packer agrees, especially regarding the individual culpability of human beings. "God's wrath in the Bible is something which men choose for themselves. Before hell is an experience inflicted by God, it is a state for which man himself opts, by retreating from the light which God shines in his heart to lead him to Himself."[3]

The doctrines of hell and eternal punishment have become increasingly unpopular in our day, even among some Christian pastors and theologians. Those who question the doctrine ought to consider that some of our clearest statements on it come from the Lord Jesus Himself (Matthew 18:8; 23:15,33; 25:41,46; Mark 9:46; compare with Revelation 14:10; 19:20; 20:10).

Books Will Be Opened

Our text tells us that books will be opened at this judgment (Revelation 20:12). These books detail the lives of the unsaved. Every action, word, and even thought are "recorded" before God's omniscient eyes. These books will provide the evidence to substantiate the divine verdict of a destiny in the lake of fire. The works that will be judged will include unbelievers' actions (Matthew 16:27), their words (Matthew 12:37), and even their thoughts and motives (Luke 8:17; Romans 2:16).

We also read of another book—the book of life. The idea of a divine register containing names goes back as far as Moses's encounter with God on Mount Sinai (Exodus 32:32-33). The apostle Paul speaks of his fellow workers as those "whose names are in the book of life" (Philippians 4:3). In the book of Revelation the book of life is mentioned six times (3:5; 13:8; 17:8; 20:12,15; and 21:27), and it contains the names of all those who belong to God. In Revelation 13:8 and 21:27, the book of life is said to belong specifically to the Lamb of God, Jesus Christ.

When Christ opens the book of life at the great white throne judgment, no name of anyone present at the judgment is in it. Their names do not appear in the book of life because they have rejected the source of life—Jesus Christ. Because they have rejected the source of life, their destiny is to be cast into the lake of fire, which constitutes the "second death" and involves eternal separation from God.

Degrees of Punishment

All who participate in the great white throne judgment have a horrific destiny ahead. [4] Scripture characterizes their existence in the lake of fire as involving weeping and gnashing of teeth (Matthew 13:41-42), condemnation (Matthew 12:36-37), destruction (Philippians 1:28), eternal punishment (Matthew 25:46), separation from God's presence (2 Thessalonians 1:8-9), and tribulation and distress (Romans 2:9). Woe to all who enter the lake of fire.

Scripture also reveals, however, that there will be degrees of punishment in hell. As Bible scholar Arnold Fruchtenbaum puts it, there will be "degrees of punishment based upon degrees of sinfulness and upon greater or lesser light or knowledge and the response or lack of it to that light." [5]

Scripture provides significant support for this idea. In Matthew 11:20-24, for example, Jesus speaks of things being more tolerable for some than for others on the day of judgment. In Luke 12:47-48, Jesus spoke of the possibility of receiving a light beating versus a severe beating. Jesus also speaks of certain people who will receive a greater condemnation than others (Luke 20:47). Moreover, in John 19:11 Jesus spoke of greater and lesser sins, and thus greater guilt (see also Matthew 10:15; 16:27; Revelation 20:12-13; 22:12).

The theological backdrop to degrees of punishment is that God is perfectly just. His judgments are fair. So, for example, when Christians face Christ at the judgment seat of Christ, some will receive rewards while others will suffer loss of rewards. Christ is fair in recognizing that some Christians live faithfully on earth while others do not. His judgment of them will reflect this reality. Conversely, at the great white throne judgment, Christ is fair in recognizing that some unbelievers are more wicked than others. Hitler, for example, will be judged much more severely than a non-Christian moralist. Jesus's judgment of the unsaved will reflect their degree of wickedness.

We might summarize these judgments this way: Just as believers differ in how they respond to God's law and therefore in their reward in heaven, so unbelievers differ in their response to God's law and therefore in their punishment in hell. Just as there are degrees of reward in heaven, so there are degrees of punishment in hell. Our Lord is perfectly just in all things.

Each lost sinner will receive just what is due him, and none will be able to argue with the Lord or question His decision. As Wiersbe puts it, "At the White Throne, there will be a Judge but no jury, a prosecution but no defense, a sentence but no appeal. No one will be able to defend himself or accuse God of unrighteousness." [6]

Resurrected to Judgment

Scripture reveals that those who participate in the great white throne judgment will be resurrected for the purpose of facing the divine Judge, Jesus Christ. During His earthly ministry, Jesus soberly announced that "an hour is coming when all who are in the tombs will hear his voice and come out, those who have done good to the resurrection of life, and those who have done evil to the resurrection of judgment" (John 5:28-29). Virtually every possible location and place will yield the bodies of the unrighteous dead—the sea, Death, and Hades—and all will be resurrected.

The Bible describes two types of resurrection—the first resurrection and the second resurrection (see Revelation 20:5-6,11-15). These are not chronological resurrections, but rather types of resurrections. The first resurrection is the resurrection of Christians, and the second resurrection is the resurrection of the wicked.

It is important to grasp that even though all Christians will be resurrected in the first resurrection, not all Christians are resurrected at the same time. For example, there is one resurrection of the righteous at the rapture, before the tribulation period (1 Thessalonians 4:16; see also Job 19:25-27; Psalm 49:15; Daniel 12:2; Isaiah 26:19; John 6:39-40,44,54; 1 Corinthians 15:42). There is another such resurrection at the end of the 1000-year millennial kingdom (Revelation 20:4). These are parts of the first resurrection because they all occur before the second (final) resurrection of the wicked. For this reason, we can say that the term "first resurrection" applies to all the resurrections of the righteous, regardless of when they occur.

The second resurrection is a sobering thing to ponder. It is described in Revelation 20:13: "The sea gave up the dead who were in it, Death and Hades gave up the dead who were in them, and they were judged." The unsaved of all time—regardless of what century they lived in, whether before the time of Christ or after—will be resurrected at the end of Christ's millennial kingdom. They will then face judgment at the great white throne judgment. Tragically, the outcome of this judgment is that they will be cast alive into the lake of fire.

OUR FATHER, *we thank You that You have provided a salvation that delivers us from the great white throne judgment and an eternal destiny in hell. We know that by our own actions, we deserve eternal punishment. But You have graciously given us eternal life through Jesus Christ. We are thankful that Jesus died in our place and took our punishment. Our stain of sin has become white as snow. Because of Jesus, we have been declared righteous and reconciled to You. For this we are eternally grateful. We praise You. You are an awesome God!*

Unbelievers and
Eternal Suffering

Everyone will experience life after death. The question is not whether an individual will enter eternity, but where he or she will spend it. The one who has trusted in Christ will spend a blissful eternity with Him in heaven (Philippians 1:21-23; 2 Corinthians 5:8). The one who has rejected Him, however, will spend eternity apart from God in a place of great suffering (Matthew 25:41). That place is hell.

In the previous chapter, I noted that it has become increasingly popular today to deny that hell exists. When church historian Martin Marty was preparing a lecture on this subject to be delivered at Harvard University, he couldn't find a single entry on hell in the indexes of several scholarly journals dating back over a hundred years. He concluded that "hell disappeared and no one noticed." [1] At the time of this writing, a number of emerging church leaders are either questioning or denying hell in their books.

Meanwhile, it is amazing to ponder how the word "hell" is so flippantly used in our society. People regularly use such phrases as "all hell broke loose," "I went through hell," and "that was one hell of a game." The effect of such flippant overuse is that for many people, the word no longer carries the idea of a literal place of suffering, but is simply a metaphor of aggression or violence.

In this chapter, our goal is to consult the Scriptures on this important and sobering topic.

What Is Hell?

The Scriptures assure us that hell is a real place. But hell was not part of God's original creation, which He called good (Genesis 1). Hell was created later to accommodate the banishment of Satan and his fallen angels, who rebelled against God (Matthew 25:41). Human beings who reject Christ will join Satan and his fallen angels in this infernal place of suffering.

In some versions of the Old Testament, including the King James, the New King James, and The Message, the word "hell" translates the Hebrew word "Sheol." Sheol can have different meanings in different contexts. Sometimes the word means "grave." Other times it refers to the place of departed people in contrast to the state of living people. The Old Testament portrays Sheol as a place of horror (Psalm 30:9), weeping, and punishment (Job 24:19).

When we get to the New Testament, we find that a number of words relate to the doctrine of hell. It would seem that *Hades* is the New Testament counterpart to *Sheol* in the Old Testament. The rich man, during the intermediate state, endured great suffering in Hades (Luke 16:19-31).

Hades, however, is a temporary abode and will one day be cast into the lake of fire (hell). In the future, the wicked evildoers in Hades will be raised from the dead and judged at the great white throne judgment. They will then be cast into the lake of fire, which will be their permanent place of suffering throughout all eternity.

Another word related to hell is *Gehenna* (Matthew 10:28). This word has an interesting history. For several generations in ancient Israel, atrocities were committed in the Valley of the Son of Hinnom (2 Kings 23:10)—atrocities that included human sacrifices, even the sacrifice of children (2 Chronicles 28:3; 33:6; Jeremiah 32:35). These unfortunate victims were sacrificed to the false Moabite god Molech.

Eventually the valley came to be used as a public rubbish dump into which all the filth in Jerusalem was poured. Not only garbage but also the carcasses of dead animals and the corpses of criminals were thrown on the heap, where they would perpetually burn.

This place was originally called (in the Hebrew) *Gen Hinnom* ("the valley of the sons of Hinnom"). The name was eventually shortened to *Ge-Hinnom*. The Greek translation of this Hebrew phrase is *Gehenna*. It became an appropriate and graphic term for the reality of hell. Jesus Himself used the word 11 times in reference to the eternal place of suffering of unredeemed humanity.

A final word related to hell is *Tartaros* (2 Peter 2:4). This word occurs only one time in the Bible and refers to a place where certain fallen angels (demons) are confined. Most fallen angels are free to roam the earth, engaging in their destructive damage wherever they find opportunity. But these imprisoned fallen angels are not free to roam, apparently because they committed an especially heinous sin against God in the past.

In the New Testament, hell is described in a wide variety of ways.

Lake of Fire or Burning Sulfur

Revelation 19:20 informs us that the beast and the false prophet—two malevolent leaders who come into power during the future tribulation period—will be "thrown alive into the lake of fire that burns with sulfur." This takes place before the beginning of Christ's millennial kingdom—that thousand-year period following the second coming of Christ during which Christ will physically rule on earth.

It is sobering to realize that at the end of the millennial kingdom—one thousand years after the beast and the false prophet were thrown into the lake of burning sulfur—the devil himself will be "thrown into the lake of fire and sulfur where the beast and the false prophet were, and they will be tormented day and night forever and ever" (Revelation 20:10).

Notice that the beast and false prophet are not burned up or annihilated at the time the devil is thrown into the lake of burning sulfur. They are still burning after one thousand years. These sinister beings, along with unbelievers of all ages, will be tormented day and night forever (Revelation 20:14-15).

Eternal Fire

Jesus often referred to the eternal destiny of the wicked as "eternal fire." He warned His followers, "If your hand or your foot causes you to sin, cut it off and throw it away. It is better for you to enter life crippled or lame than with two hands or two feet to be thrown into the eternal fire" (Matthew 18:8).

Following His second coming, when He separates the sheep (believers) from the goats (unbelievers), Jesus will say to the goats, "Depart from me, you cursed, into the eternal fire prepared for the devil and his angels" (Matthew 25:41).

What precisely is the fire of hell? Some believe it is literal fire, and that may very well be the case. Others believe fire may be a metaphorical way of expressing the great wrath of God. Scripture informs us, "The LORD your God is a consuming fire, a jealous God" (Deuteronomy 4:24). "Our God is a consuming fire" (Hebrews 12:29). "His wrath is poured out like fire" (Nahum 1:6). "Who can stand when he appears? For he is like a refiner's fire" (Malachi 3:2). God said His wrath will "go forth like fire, and burn with none to quench it" (Jeremiah 4:4). How awful is the fiery wrath of God!

Fiery Furnace

Scripture sometimes refers to the destiny of the wicked as the "fiery furnace." Jesus said that at the end of the age the holy angels will gather all evildoers and "throw them into the fiery furnace. In that place there will be weeping and gnashing of teeth" (Matthew 13:42).

There is a difference between fiery furnaces on earth and the fiery furnace of hell. On earth, when one throws debris into a furnace, the debris is utterly consumed. The debris turns to ashes. This is not the case for those who suffer eternally in hell, for they never turn to ashes. They are not annihilated. This is a terrible thing to ponder, but the Scriptures are clear that the wicked suffer eternally in hell (Mark 9:47-48).

What is meant by "weeping and gnashing of teeth"? "Weeping" carries the idea of "wailing, not merely with tears, but with every outward expression of grief." [2] The weeping will be caused by the environment, the company, the remorse and guilt, and the shame that is part and parcel of hell.

People "gnash their teeth" when they are angry, as British evangelist John Blanchard explains in his well-received book *Whatever Happened to Hell?*

> The wicked will be angry at the things which gave them pleasure on earth but now give them pain in hell; angry at the sins that wrecked their lives; angry at themselves for being who they are; angry at Satan and his helpers for producing the temptations which led them into sin; and, even while compelled to acknowledge his glory and goodness, angry at God for condemning them to this dreadful state. [3]

Destruction

Jesus warned in Matthew 7:13, "Enter by the narrow gate. For the gate is wide and the way is easy that leads to destruction, and those who enter by it are many." The ultimate destruction to which Jesus refers is the destruction wrought in hell.

Second Thessalonians 1:8-9 tells us that there will be "vengeance on those who do not know God and on those who do not obey the gospel of our Lord Jesus. They will suffer the punishment of eternal destruction, away from the presence of the Lord and from the glory of his might."

The Greek word translated "destruction" in this verse carries the meaning "sudden ruin," or "loss of all that gives worth to existence." The word does not refer to annihilation, but to separation from God and a loss of everything worthwhile in life. Just as "endless life" belongs to Christians, so "endless destruction" belongs to those opposed to Christ. [4]

Eternal Punishment

Jesus affirmed that the wicked "will go away into eternal punishment, but the righteous into eternal life" (Matthew 25:46). Notice that the eternality of the punishment of the wicked equals the eternality of the life of the righteous. One is just as long as the other. This shows that the punishment of the wicked lasts forever. It never ceases.

The eternal nature of this punishment is emphasized all through-out Scripture. The fire of hell, for example, is called an "unquenchable fire" (Mark 9:43). The worm of the wicked "does not die" (Mark 9:48). The "smoke of their [sinners'] torment goes up forever and ever" (Revelation 14:11).

Of particular significance is the reference in Revelation 20:10 to the devil, the beast, and the false prophet being tormented in the lake of fire "forever and ever." This is significant because the Greek word translated "forever and ever" is used elsewhere in Revelation in reference to the endless worship of God (1:6; 4:9; 5:13). The word is also used of the endless life of God (4:10; 10:6). Further, the word is used in reference to Christ's endless kingdom (11:15). The suffering of evildoers is endless...endless...endless.

Endless Exclusion from God's Presence

Unquestionably the greatest pain suffered by those in hell is that they are forever excluded from the presence of God. If ecstatic joy is found in the presence of God (Psalm 16:11), then utter dismay is found in His absence.

At the future judgment, some will actually claim to be Christians and will claim to have served Christ during their years on earth. But Christ will say to them, "I do not know where you come from. Depart from me, all you workers of evil!" (Luke 13:27). Such individuals will find themselves forever excluded from God's presence. They will forever be "away from the presence of the Lord" (2 Thessalonians 1:8-9).

At the judgment of the sheep (believers) and goats (unbelievers), Christ will command the goats, "Depart from me, you cursed, into the eternal fire prepared for the devil and his angels" (Matthew 25:41). What utterly horrific words to hear from the lips of the divine Judge!

> OUR FATHER, *we know it is not Your desire for people to end up in hell. We are aware that You are "not wishing that any should perish, but that all should reach repentance." We recognize that You take no pleasure in the death of the wicked. Our*

understanding of what Scripture says about hell renews our moti-
vation to reach the lost. Enable us, O Lord, to boldly participate
in fulfilling the Great Commission to reach all nations with the
gospel message. Empower us to effectively contend for the faith
that was once for all handed down to the saints.
We praise You, O Lord.

No Second Chance
After Death

We can understand why some today believe there must be a second chance to turn to God following the moment of death. After all, they reason, God is characterized by love. Surely in His compassion He will give those who reject Christ another chance beyond death's door to become believers despite their sinful and rebellious lives on earth.

Such a view may sound appealing to human reasoning, but I think it goes against the clear teachings of Scripture. Two passages in 1 Peter, however, are sometimes misinterpreted to teach a second chance—3:18-19 and 4:6. Let's take a brief look at these verses.

1 Peter 3:18-19

In 1 Peter 3:18-19 we read, "Christ also suffered once for sins, the righteous for the unrighteous, that he might bring us to God, being put to death in the flesh but made alive in the spirit, in which he went and proclaimed to the spirits in prison." The King James Version renders the latter part of the verse, "he went and preached unto the spirits in prison." Some people reason that if spirits in the afterlife can be preached to, they must be able to respond to the gospel and become believers in the afterlife. This implies there is a second chance for everyone to believe in God in the afterlife.

Such a view is untenable. Many evangelical scholars believe that the "spirits in prison" referred to in this passage are not the souls of unbelieving people but are rather fallen angels—demonic spirits who grievously sinned against God. Some believe these spirits are the apparent fallen angels ("sons of God") of Genesis 6:1-6, who were disobedient to God during the days of Noah. This same group of evil angels is apparently alluded to in 2 Peter 2:4-5 and Jude 6. According to this interpretation, these evil angels disobeyed God, left their proper angelic realm, and somehow entered into sexual relations with human women.

The Greek word rendered "preach" (*kerusso*) in the King James translation of 1 Peter 3:19 is not the word typically used for preaching the gospel, but rather points to a proclamation, as in a proclamation of victory. This passage may imply that the powers of darkness thought they had destroyed Jesus at the crucifixion, but in raising Him from the dead, God turned the tables on them, and Jesus Himself proclaimed their doom. If this is the correct interpretation, it is clear that the verse has nothing to do with human spirits hearing and responding to the gospel in the afterlife.

Other Bible expositors hold to a different view. They suggest that Jesus, between His death and resurrection, went to the place of the dead and "preached" to the wicked contemporaries of Noah (those who rejected and even mocked Noah as a prophet of God). This preaching, however, was not a gospel message but was rather a proclamation of victory.

Still other Bible expositors believe this passage refers to Christ preaching through the person of Noah to those who, because they rejected his message, are now spirits in prison. One must keep in mind that 1 Peter 1:11 tells us that the Spirit of Christ spoke through the Old Testament prophets. And Noah is later described as a herald (or preacher) of righteousness (2 Peter 2:5). So the Spirit of Christ may have preached through Noah to the ungodly humans who, much later, at the time of Peter's writing, were now "spirits in prison" awaiting final judgment.

Regardless of which of the above interpretations is correct, evangelical scholars unanimously agree that this passage does not teach that people can hear and respond to the gospel in the next life. They say this because of the preponderance of Bible passages that teach that those who refuse to turn to Christ by faith in this present life are irrevocably consigned to a destiny in the lake of fire (for example, Matthew 25:46; Revelation 20:15).

1 Peter 4:6

"This is why the gospel was preached even to those who are dead, that though judged in the flesh the way people are, they might live in the spirit the way God does." This verse is also sometimes interpreted to mean that humans might have a second chance after death.

This is a difficult verse to interpret. A prime principle of Bible interpretation, however, is that we ought always to interpret difficult verses in light of what the clearer verses teach. The clearer verses, some of which I'll address below, teach that our decision for or against God is determined in this one life.

Evangelical Bible expositors have offered several interpretations of this verse, but perhaps the best view is that the verse refers to those who are now dead but who heard the gospel while they were yet alive. This makes sense in view of the tenses used: The gospel was preached (in the past) to those who are dead (presently).

In interpreting these words from 1 Peter, it is good to keep in mind the words of Jesus in Luke 16:19-31. Once the rich man had died and ended up in a place of great suffering, he had no further opportunity for redemption. Nothing could be done at that point to ease his situation at all (verse 24). No gospel was preached to him. He seemed to accept the finality of his situation, which is why he wanted to warn his brothers still alive on earth so that they would not have to suffer the same final destiny. (Of course, he was prohibited from contacting his still-living brothers.)

Now Is the Day of Salvation

Hebrews 9:27 affirms that "it is appointed for man to die once, and after that comes judgment." Notice the order of events. The text does not say that man dies, has a second chance to believe, and then faces judgment. Rather, it says that man dies and then faces the judgment.

Recall also that the primary basis of judgment throughout Scripture has to do with one's behavior during earthly life. Revelation 20:12 tells

us that "the dead were judged…according to what they had done"—
that is, what they had done during earthly life. Ecclesiastes 12:14 likewise affirms that "God will bring every deed into judgment, with every
secret thing, whether good or evil." What deeds? Deeds done during
earthly life. If there were a second chance after death, such verses could
not be taken seriously.

The fact that we die once and then face the judgment is one reason
for the apostle Paul's urgency in 2 Corinthians 6:2: "Now is the favor-
able time; behold, now is the day of salvation." No one should wait to
respond to the gospel, for death could come at any time. This short life
on earth is the only time we have to decide for or against Christ. Once
we die, there is no further opportunity (or second chance) to believe
in Jesus for salvation.

Ecclesiastes 9:12 tells us that "man does not know his time [of
death]. Like fish that are taken in an evil net, and like birds that are
caught in a snare, so the children of man are snared at an evil time,
when it suddenly falls upon them." If this passage tells us anything, it
tells us that death often comes suddenly, without warning. The impli-
cation is that we must be prepared for the moment, for there are no
second chances. A sense of urgency would be unnecessary if we have a
second chance following death.

We see this wisdom in Proverbs 27:1: "Do not boast about tomorrow, for you do not know what a day may bring." Each new day may
bring the prospect of death. It is therefore wise to turn to Christ for
salvation while there is yet time, for there are no second chances in the
afterlife. There is no possibility of redemption beyond death's door.

Many people rationalize that they'll have plenty of time to turn to
the Lord later in life, so they don't need to bother with salvation matters at the present time. Such a view is full of folly. Consider Jesus's
words in Luke 12:16-21.

> The land of a rich man produced plentifully, and he thought
> to himself, "What shall I do, for I have nowhere to store
> my crops?" And he said, "I will do this: I will tear down my
> barns and build larger ones, and there I will store all my

grain and my goods. And I will say to my soul, 'Soul, you have ample goods laid up for many years; relax, eat, drink, be merry.'" But God said to him, "Fool! This night your soul is required of you, and the things you have prepared, whose will they be?" So is the one who lays up treasure for himself and is not rich toward God.

Many people today live as if they're entitled to 70 or 80 years. They don't plan on dying younger. Accordingly, they don't take the gospel of Jesus Christ seriously. The reality is that many die young and are unprepared for death and what lies beyond. Again, then, "Now is the day of salvation."

Recall the teaching of 2 Peter 2:9: "The Lord knows how…to keep the unrighteous under punishment until the day of judgment." Notice that no second chance is found anywhere in this verse. The wicked who die are kept in a place of punishment while they await the future great white throne judgment, after which they will be consigned to the lake of fire (Revelation 20:11-15).

I therefore must say it again: Now is the day of salvation!

OUR FATHER, *we ask that You would lift the veil of blindness that seems to keep so many from recognizing the urgency of turning to Christ for salvation this very day. We also recognize our own failures in urgently communicating the gospel to others. Please enable us to be more effective witnesses of the gospel of Jesus Christ. Put a desire in our hearts to be "fishers of men," recognizing that there are no second chances for people to be saved in the afterlife.*

Hooking Our Hope
in Heaven

My friends, I've talked a lot in this book about what happens after life. As we draw to a close in this chapter, I want to exhort you to live in light of eternity.

Think about it. In view of what happens after life, what happens on earth takes on more urgency. The years that we have on this tiny dot of a planet can never be recovered. And the way we use our short years on earth has profound implications for the afterlife. We must therefore use these fast-passing years with purpose and resolve.

God is the One who created time. When God created the earth and put human beings on it, He set boundaries for day and night (Job 26:10) and divided the year into seasons (Genesis 1:14). These are "handles" by which we humans can orient ourselves as time passes. As the days continually pass, so seasons eventually pass, and as seasons pass, so years eventually pass. And as years pass, we eventually die and enter into eternity. Today we live in time but for eternity.

We Live in Time but for Eternity

Eternity is a big concept. We read in the pages of Holy Writ that God has "put eternity into man's heart" (Ecclesiastes 3:11). As one Christian leader put it, "Within each of us is an inner sense or feeling that death is not the end, but that there must be something beyond the grave. Even if we deny it or ignore it, this inner yearning is still there—and it is universal. Where did it come from? The Bible says God placed it within us."[1]

Though we live in a world of time, we have intimations of eternity in our hearts. We instinctively think of "forever." We seem to intrinsically realize that beyond this life lies the possibility of a shoreless ocean of time. It is wondrous to even think about it. One Christian wrote that this sense of eternity in the human heart makes us heaven-bent, that our hearts have an "inner tilt upward" and that the grain of our souls "leans heavenward."[2]

From the first book in the Bible to the last, we read of great men and women of God who demonstrated that eternity permeated their hearts. We read of people like Abel, Enoch, Noah, Abraham, and David... each yearning to live with God in eternity.

David put it this way: "As a deer pants for flowing streams, so pants my soul for you, O God. My soul thirsts for God, for the living God. When shall I come and appear before God?" (Psalm 42:1-2). He exulted, "I shall dwell in the house of the LORD forever" (Psalm 23:6).

Moses is another great example.

> By faith Moses, when he was grown up, refused to be called the son of Pharaoh's daughter, choosing rather to be mistreated with the people of God than to enjoy the fleeting pleasures of sin. He considered the reproach of Christ greater wealth than the treasures of Egypt, for he was looking to the reward. By faith he left Egypt, not being afraid of the anger of the king, for he endured as seeing him who is invisible (Hebrews 11:24-27).

It is interesting that the writer of Hebrews said Moses "considered the reproach of Christ greater wealth than the treasures of Egypt" because Moses lived at least 1500 years before Christ. It is difficult to ascertain how much Moses knew about Christ, but our text clearly indicates that Moses forsook Egypt because he had a personal faith in Christ. God had apparently revealed to him things invisible to the natural eye. Moses became aware of another King, another kingdom, and a better reward.

The Hebrew word translated "considered" in this passage indicates careful thought and not a quick decision. Moses thought through his decision, weighing the pros and cons. He weighed what Egypt had to offer against the promises of God for the future. He came to the conclusion that what God offered in eternity was far superior to anything Egypt could offer for the future. Moses thus lived with eternity in view. He made his decisions based on how they would impact his existence in the afterlife. If we were to try to reconstruct Moses's reasoning, we might come up with something such as this.

> Yahweh-God has revealed future things to me, invisible things, but things of glory, heavenly things. I believe what He says. At the same time He has made known to me that I am His chosen instrument to deliver His people, my brethren according to the flesh, from bondage. But I am the adopted son of Pharaoh's daughter. To me the throne of Egypt has been promised, as heir through her. If I follow God's program for me, I must suffer reproach, the reproach of the Messiah, the Deliverer. If, on the other hand, I remain in the royal court, all the wealth of Egypt is mine—and how great is that wealth! If I take the course Yahweh has laid out for me, I must suffer affliction with my brethren, and I have seen how heavy their burdens are. Whereas if I am ready to be called Pharaoh's grandson, the pleasures of all that Egypt has to offer, the pleasures of sin, may be enjoyed. Each of these things—the affliction of the people of God, and the pleasures of sin—is temporal. I am looking to life after death. Then, he who has suffered within the will of God will be rewarded; but he who has followed the way of the flesh will be judged. What God has spoken is surely true. I make my choice. I refuse to be called the son of Pharaoh's daughter, preferring by choice to suffer affliction with God's people than to enjoy the pleasures of sin, accounting the reproach of the Messiah, with its present satisfaction and eventual reward, greater riches by far than the treasures of Egypt. [3]

Moses would certainly have agreed with what the apostle Paul wrote many centuries later: "This light momentary affliction is preparing for us an eternal weight of glory beyond all comparison, as we look not to the things that are seen but to the things that are unseen. For the things that are seen are transient, but the things that are unseen are eternal" (2 Corinthians 4:17-18).

Moses gave up temporal pleasure for the sake of his Savior, Jesus Christ. His priorities were as they should have been. And what joy Moses's commitment must have brought to the heart of God! Do you not sense within your heart a calling to follow Moses's lead in this regard?

Jonathan Edwards seemed to mirror Moses's commitment. Edwards, who lived from 1703 to 1758, was in the Puritan habit of framing spiritual resolutions to discipline himself. George Marsden, author of the wonderful book *Jonathan Edwards: A Life*, tells us that "in a number of them he reminded himself, as he had been taught since childhood, to think of his own dying, or to live as though he had only an hour left before his death or 'before I should hear the last trump.'" [4] Edwards commented that "it becomes us to spend this life only as a journey toward heaven…to which we should subordinate all other concerns of life. Why should we labor for or set our hearts on anything else, but that which is our proper end and true happiness?" [5] He thus made and sought to keep the following resolutions (among many others):

- "Resolved, to endeavor to obtain for myself as much happiness, in the other world, as I possibly can."

- "Resolved, that I will live so as I shall wish I had done when I come to die."

- "Resolved, to endeavor to my utmost to act as I can think I should do, if, I had already seen the happiness of heaven, and hell's torments." [6]

Billy Graham agrees with this perspective. "The more seriously we take Heaven, the more seriously we'll take our responsibilities here on earth. Life is short; none of us knows how long we have. Live each day as if it were your last—for someday it will be." [7]

The Amount of Time We Have Is in God's Hands

Each of us has an innate desire to live as long as possible. That is natural. But the actual timing of our deaths is in the hands of our sovereign God. He has allotted a certain amount of time on earth for each of us. As Job affirmed to God, man's "days are determined, and the number of his months is with you, and you have appointed his limits that he cannot pass" (Job 14:5).

Scripture reveals that God himself "made from one man every nation of mankind to live on all the face of the earth, having determined allotted periods and the boundaries of their dwelling place" (Acts 17:26). The backdrop to this New Testament affirmation seems to be an Old Testament psalm: "In your book were written, every one of them, the days that were formed for me, when as yet there were none of them" (Psalm 139:16).

Of course, we Christians never need to fear the day death will come. Our God, who loves us infinitely, is in charge of the timing of our rendezvous with death, and we can trust Him completely. With the psalmist, we can restfully affirm, "My times are in your hand" (Psalm 31:15). We can count on the fact that we are immortal up until the time we have accomplished all that God intends for us to accomplish. Once that work is complete, God calls us home!

Previously in the book I noted that some people experience what many call an "untimely death." When a young person dies in a car wreck, for example, we say that this person's death was untimely. From a scriptural perspective, however, there are no untimely deaths, for all deaths occur according to God's sovereign timing (Isaiah 46:10; Acts 2:23; Ephesians 1:11). We can take great comfort in this truth, for when a Christian loved one dies, we can rest assured that he or she has died according to God's precise sovereign timing. Yes, we still mourn (1 Thessalonians 4:13), but our grief is tempered by our awareness of

God's sovereign oversight of all earthly affairs (Psalms 21:1; 22:28; Jeremiah 1:5; Jonah 1:17; Matthew 6:26; Acts 12:7-11; Romans 13:1).

Use Time Wisely

The knowledge we have gained about heaven in this book should not be an end in itself. Rather, it should influence the way we live and use our time in the present. These tiny years here on earth have a destiny that can never be repeated. We are at our best when we use our available time the way the Lord wants us to, as the following Scriptures attest.

- "Look carefully then how you walk, not as unwise but as wise, making the best use of the time, because the days are evil. Therefore do not be foolish, but understand what the will of the Lord is" (Ephesians 5:15-17).

- "Walk in wisdom toward outsiders, making the best use of the time" (Colossians 4:5).

- "Teach us to number our days that we may get a heart of wisdom" (Psalm 90:12).

- Pray "at all times in the Spirit, with all prayer and supplication. To that end keep alert with all perseverance, making supplication for all the saints" (Ephesians 6:18).

- "So then, as we have opportunity, let us do good to everyone, and especially to those who are of the household of faith" (Galatians 6:10).

- "O LORD, make me know my end and what is the measure of my days; let me know how fleeting I am!" (Psalm 39:4).

- "Blessed are they who observe justice, who do righteousness at all times!" (Psalm 106:3).

OUR FATHER, *thank You for the gift of time. We regret those many occasions when we've used time wastefully or unwisely.*

*May it never happen again! Please move our hearts to resolve to
use our time wisely. And may the realities of heaven motivate us to
use every moment on earth in a Christ-honoring way. With each
day that passes, we are one day closer to being with You in heaven.
We are thankful for the heavenly destiny that awaits us.
We praise You, O Lord.*

Bibliography

Alcorn, Randy. *Heaven*. Wheaton, IL: Tyndale House, 2004.

Ankerberg, John, and John Weldon. *The Facts on Life After Death*. Eugene, OR: Harvest House, 1992.

Baxter, J. Sidlow. *The Other Side of Death*. Grand Rapids, MI: Kregel, 1997.

Baxter, Richard. *The Saints' Everlasting Rest*. Philadelphia, PA: Lippincott, 1859.

Boa, Kenneth, and Robert Bowman. *Sense and Nonsense about Heaven and Hell*. Grand Rapids, MI: Zondervan, 2007.

Buchanan, Mark. *Things Unseen: Living in Light of Forever*. Sisters, OR: Multnomah, 2002.

Connelly, Douglas. *What the Bible Really Says: After Life*. Downers Grove, IL: InterVarsity Press, 1995.

Enns, Paul. *Heaven Revealed: What Is It Like? What Will We Do?...And 11 Other Things You've Wondered About*. Chicago, IL: Moody, 2011.

Graham, Billy. *Death and the Life After*. Nashville, TN: Thomas Nelson, 2009.

_____. *The Heaven Answer Book*. Nashville, TN: Thomas Nelson, 2012.

_____. *Nearing Home: Life, Faith, and Finishing Well*. Nashville, TN: Thomas Nelson, 2011.

Habermas, Gary R., and J.P. Moreland. *Immortality: The Other Side of Death*. Nashville, TN: Thomas Nelson, 1992.

Hitchcock, Mark. *55 Answers to Questions About Life After Death*. Sisters, OR: Multnomah Books, 2005.

Hoekema, Anthony A. *The Bible and the Future*. Grand Rapids, MI: Eerdmans, 1984.

Hoyt, Herman A. *The End Times*. Chicago, IL: Moody Press, 1969.

Ladd, George Eldon. *The Last Things*. Grand Rapids, MI: Eerdmans, 1982.

Lotz, Anne Graham. *Heaven: My Father's House*. Nashville, TN: Thomas Nelson, 2001.

MacArthur, John. *Because the Time Is Near*. Chicago, IL: Moody Books, 2007.

_____. *The Glories of Heaven*. Wheaton, IL: Crossway Books, 1996.

McGrath, Alister. *A Brief History of Heaven*. Malden, MA: Blackwell, 2003.

Morrow, Barry. *Heaven Observed*. Colorado Springs, CO: NavPress, 2001.

Pache, Rene. *The Future Life*. Chicago, IL: Moody Press, 1980.

Pentecost, J. Dwight. *Things to Come*. Grand Rapids, MI: Zondervan, 1974.

Rhodes, Ron. *Angels Among Us: Separating Truth from Fiction*. Eugene, OR: Harvest House, 1995.

_____. *Heaven: The Undiscovered Country*. Eugene, OR: Harvest House, 1996.

_____. *The Wonder of Heaven*. Eugene, OR: Harvest House, 2009.

Ryle, J.C. *Heaven*. Great Britain: Christian Focus, 2001.

Sanders, J. Oswald. *Heaven: Better by Far*. Grand Rapids, MI: Discovery House, 1993.

Sauer, Eric. *From Eternity to Eternity*. Grand Rapids, MI: Eerdmans, 1979.

Smith, Wilbur M. *The Biblical Doctrine of Heaven*. Chicago, IL: Moody Press, 1974.

Tada, Joni Eareckson. *Heaven: Your Real Home*. Grand Rapids, MI: Zondervan, 1995.

Wright, Rusty. *The Other Side of Life*. San Bernardino, CA: Here's Life, 1979.

Zodhiates, Spiros. *Life After Death*. Chattanooga, TN: AMG, 1989.

Notes

Chapter 1: An Appointed Time to Die

1. Thomas L. Constable, *Notes on Acts*. See notes on 17:26. Available online at soniclight.com/con stable/notes/pdf/acts.pdf.

2. Paul Enns, *Heaven Revealed: What Is It Like? What Will We Do?...And 11 Other Things You've Wondered About* (Chicago: Moody, 2011), p. 48.

Chapter 2: Death: A Transition into the Afterlife

1. See William B. Brahms, *Last Words of Notable People: Final Words of More Than 3500 Noteworthy People Throughout History* (Haddonfield: Reference Desk Press, 2010).

2. J. Vernon McGee, *Thru the Bible with J. Vernon McGee*, vol. 2, *Joshua–Psalms* (Nashville: Thomas Nelson, 1984). See notes on Psalm 23.

3. Warren Wiersbe, *With the Word Bible Commentary* (Nashville: Thomas Nelson, 1993), p. 504.

4. John Gill, *Gill's Bible Commentary* (Osnova, 2012). See notes on 2 Corinthians 5:8.

5. Paul Enns, *Heaven Revealed: What Is It Like? What Will We Do?...And 11 Other Things You've Wondered About* (Chicago: Moody, 2011), p. 46.

Chapter 3: The Intermediate State

1. Warren Wiersbe, *The Wiersbe Bible Commentary: New Testament* (Colorado Springs: David C. Cook, 2007), p. 515.

Chapter 4: The Rapture: A Rendezvous with the Lord in the Air

1. Thomas L. Constable, *Notes on 1 Corinthians*. See notes on 15:51-52. Available online at sonic light.com/constable/notes/pdf/1corinthians.pdf.

2. Warren Wiersbe, *The Wiersbe Bible Commentary: New Testament* (Colorado Springs: David C. Cook, 2007), p. 793.

Chapter 6: Christians at the Judgment Seat of Christ

1. *The ESV Study Bible* (Wheaton: Crossway, 2009). See notes on 1 Corinthians 3:14-15.

Chapter 7: New Heavens and a New Earth

1. John MacArthur, *MacArthur New Testament Commentary*, vol. 20, *Romans 1–8* (Chicago: Moody, 1991), p. 455.

2. David Walls, *1 and 2 Peter, 1, 2, and 3 John, Jude*, vol. 11 of *Holman Bible Commentary*, ed. Max Anders (Nashville: Holman Reference, 2001). See notes on 2 Peter 3:5-7.

3. Randy Alcorn, *Heaven* (Wheaton: Tyndale House, 2004), p. 88.

Chapter 12: Face-to-Face Fellowship with God

1. bible.org/illustration/testimony-125-ad.

Chapter 13: A Reunion of Christian Loved Ones

1. Paul Enns, *Heaven Revealed* (Chicago: Moody, 2011), p. 43.

Chapter 14: Meaningful Activities in Heaven

1. Warren Wiersbe, *The Wiersbe Bible Commentary: New Testament* (Colorado Springs: David C. Cook, 2007), p. 204.

2. *Thomas Constable, Notes on Luke.* See notes at 19:27. Available online at soniclight.com/constable/notes/pdf/luke.pdf.

3. For example, see John D. Morris, "Will We Have Any Work to Do in Heaven?" Available online at www.icr.org/article/2327/.

Chapter 17: Assessing Personal Visits to Heaven

1. Rodney Clapp, "Rumors of Heaven," *Christianity Today*, October 7, 1988, p. 20.

2. William MacDonald, *Believer's Bible Commentary*, ed. Arthur L. Farstad (Nashville: Thomas Nelson, 1995). See notes on 2 Corinthians 12:4.

3. Todd Burpo and Lynn Vincent, *Heaven Is for Real: A Little Boy's Astounding Story of His Trip to Heaven and Back* (Nashville: Thomas Nelson, 2010), p. 149.

4. John Ankerberg and John Weldon, *The Facts on Life After Death* (Eugene: Harvest House, 1992), pp. 10-11.

5. Cited in Ankerberg and Weldon, p. 21.

6. Jerry Yamamoto, "The Near-Death Experience," *Christian Research Journal*, Spring 1992, p. 5.

7. Yamamoto, p. 5.

8. Gary R. Habermas and J.P. Moreland, *Immortality: The Other Side of Death* (Nashville: Thomas Nelson, 1992), p. 93.

Chapter 18: Unbelievers at the Great White Throne Judgment

1. Charles Ryrie, *A Survey of Bible Doctrine* (Chicago: Moody Press, 1972), chapter 9, "What Does the Future Hold?"

2. Warren Wiersbe, *The Wiersbe Bible Commentary: New Testament* (Colorado Springs: David C. Cook, 2007), p. 1097.

3. J.I. Packer, *Knowing God* (Downers Grove: InterVarsity, 1973), p. 138.

4. Charles Ryrie, *Basic Theology: A Popular Systematic Guide to Understanding Biblical Truth* (Chicago: Moody Press, 1999), chapter 99, "Future Judgments."

5. Arnold Fruchtenbaum, *The Footsteps of the Messiah: A Study of the Sequence of Prophetic Events* (Tustin: Ariel Ministries, 2003), chapter 21, "The Aftermath."

6. Warren Wiersbe, *The Wiersbe Bible Exposition Commentary: New Testament*, vol. 2 (Colorado Springs: Chariot Victor, 1992), p. 621.

Chapter 19: Unbelievers and Eternal Suffering

1. Cited in John Blanchard, *Whatever Happened to Hell?* (Durham, England: Evangelical Press, 1993), p. 13.
2. Blanchard, p. 156.
3. Blanchard, p. 156.
4. Robert L. Thomas, *Ephesians, Philippians, Colossians, 1, 2 Thessalonians, 1, 2 Timothy, Titus, Philemon*, vol. 11 of *The Expositor's Bible Commentary*, ed. Frank E. Gaebelein (Grand Rapids: Zondervan, 1978), p. 313.

Chapter 21: Hooking Our Hope in Heaven

1. Billy Graham, *Nearing Home: Faith, Life, and Finishing Well* (Nashville: Thomas Nelson, 2011), p. 168.
2. Mark Buchanan, *Things Unseen: Living in Light of Forever* (Sisters: Multnomah Books, 2006), p. 11.
3. E. Schuyler English, *Studies in the Epistle to the Hebrews* (Neptune: Loizeaux Brothers, 1976), p. 406.
4. George Marsden, *Jonathan Edwards: A Life* (New Haven: Yale University Press, 2003), p. 51.
5. Cited in Randy Alcorn, *Heaven* (Wheaton: Tyndale House, 2004), p. 5.
6. Cited in Alcorn, p. 28.
7. Billy Graham, *The Heaven Answer Book* (Nashville: Thomas Nelson, 2012), p. 159.

Other Great Harvest House Books
by Ron Rhodes

BOOKS ABOUT THE BIBLE

The Big Book of Bible Answers
Bite-Size Bible® Answers
Bite-Size Bible® Charts
Bite-Size Bible® Definitions
Bite-Size Bible® Handbook
Commonly Misunderstood Bible Verses
The Complete Guide to Bible Translations
Find It Fast in the Bible
The Popular Dictionary of Bible Prophecy
Understanding the Bible from A to Z
What Does the Bible Say About…?

BOOKS ABOUT THE END TIMES

40 Days Through Revelation
Cyber Meltdown
The End Times in Chronological Order
Northern Storm Rising
Unmasking the Antichrist

BOOKS ABOUT OTHER IMPORTANT TOPICS

5-Minute Apologetics for Today
1001 Unforgettable Quotes About God, Faith, and the Bible
Angels Among Us
Answering the Objections of Atheists,
Agnostics, and Skeptics
Christianity According to the Bible
The Complete Guide to Christian Denominations
Conversations with Jehovah's Witnesses
Find It Quick Handbook on Cults and New Religions
The Truth Behind Ghosts, Mediums, and Psychic Phenomena
What Happens After Life?
Why Do Bad Things Happen If God Is Good?

THE 10 MOST IMPORTANT THINGS SERIES

The 10 Most Important Things You Can Say to a Catholic

The 10 Most Important Things You Can Say to a Jehovah's Witness

The 10 Most Important Things You Can Say to a Mason

The 10 Most Important Things You Can Say to a Mormon

The 10 Things You Need to Know About Islam

The 10 Things You Should Know About the Creation vs. Evolution Debate

QUICK REFERENCE GUIDES

Halloween: What You Need to Know

Islam: What You Need to Know

Jehovah's Witnesses: What You Need to Know

THE REASONING FROM THE SCRIPTURES SERIES

Reasoning from the Scriptures with Catholics

Reasoning from the Scriptures with the Jehovah's Witnesses

Reasoning from the Scriptures with Masons

Reasoning from the Scriptures with the Mormons

Reasoning from the Scriptures with Muslims

LITTLE BOOKS

Little Book About God

Little Book About Heaven

Little Book About the Bible

To learn more about Harvest House books and
to read sample chapters, visit our website:

www.harvesthousepublishers.com

HARVEST HOUSE PUBLISHERS
EUGENE, OREGON